ONE LORD ONE SPIRIT ONE BODY

*Ecumenical Grace
of the
Charismatic
Movement*

by Peter D. Hocken

Co-Published by

The Word Among Us Press
Gaithersburg, Maryland U.S.A.

The Paternoster Press
Exeter, Devon, Great Britain

Grateful acknowledgement is made to the following for permission to use copyrighted material:

Bridge Publishing Company—*Nine O'Clock in the Morning* by Dennis Bennett

Lutheran Charismatic Renewal Services——*The Charismatic Renewal Among Lutherans* by Larry Christenson

Paulist Press—*Catholic Pentecostals* by Kevin and Dorothy Ranaghan

Paternoster Press—*Streams of Renewal* by Peter Hocken

The Scripture quotations contained herein are from the Revised Standard Version Bible, Catholic Edition, copyright 1965 and 1966 by the Division of Christian Education of the National Council of the Churches of Christ in the USA, and are used by permission.

All other quotations in Chapter One are taken from *Trinity* magazine.

The Word Among Us Press
P.O. Box 2427
Gaithersburg, MD 20879

This edition published by arrangement with The Paternoster Press, Exeter, UK.

CONTENTS

FOREWORD

IN RECENT YEARS, THE WORK OF PETER HOCKEN HAS GAINED increasing recognition and influence in Pentecostal and Charismatic circles. Brought up an Anglican in England, he was in his youth a convert to the Roman Catholic Church. In 1971 he was introduced to Catholic charismatic renewal and was baptized in the Holy Spirit. At this time he was deeply influenced by attending services in a multi-racial Pentecostal congregation in Birmingham, England. Here he saw a powerful expression of New Testament Christianity which he instinctively recognized as a "naked grace" for the entire body of Christ. From this experience, he became a fast friend of the Classical Pentecostals.

After being baptized in the Holy Spirit, he devoted himself to the study and propagation of the charismatic renewal in all the churches, including his own Roman Catholic Church. Since 1976, he has lived and worked in the Mother of God Community in Gaithersburg, Maryland. There he has been part of a living fellowship, that has blessed the wider church with *The Word Among Us*, a daily biblical prayer guide that has gained a wide circulation since its introduction in 1981. This publication reflects the major attention given to biblical studies and devotions among Catholics in the renewal.

His years in the Mother of God Community have sharpened his appreciation for the "baptism in the Holy Spirit" as well as for the treasures of the traditional church. Much of his more recent work has been shaped by his shared life in the community, knowing the truth of the words of the psalmist, "How good and pleasant it is when brothers dwell in unity" (Psalm 133:1). This has helped form his historical and theological studies which in turn have enriched the charismatic movement as a whole.

In many ways, Hocken's life is an example of the type of ecumenism he proclaims. Loved and respected in his own church, he is also highly regarded in others as well. A measure of the respect in which Hocken is held was his election in 1985 to be the first Roman Catholic president of the Society for Pentecostal Studies, a group made up primarily of Classical Pentecostals.

In *One Lord One Spirit One Body*, Hocken has tackled the difficult problem of ecumenical relations among those who have been touched by the renewal. His practical and scriptural guidelines should be welcome to everyone who works for the Lord in the renewal. His major burden is to avoid the extremes of "denominationalism" on the one hand, and "non-denominationalism" on the other, both of which he sees as detrimental to the unity of believers. In this book he points to a "third way" which is truly ecumenical in that it values and respects the various Christian traditions while keeping in view the unity of the one historic church for which Christ died.

This book should be in the hands and hearts of every person involved in the charismatic renewal, especially those working in ecumenical relations and ministries. Like Peter Hocken himself, the message of this book has been touched and inspired by the Holy Spirit.

Vinson Synan
Chairman
New Orleans 1987 Congress
on the Holy Spirit and
World Evangelization

INTRODUCTION

THIS BOOK IS BASED ON A PAPER "ECUMENISM AND CHARIS-
matic Renewal" presented at the annual theological symposium of
the National Association of Diocesan Liaisons for Catholic Charismatic Renewal at Sedalia, Colorado in September, 1986. This
paper was so well received that its expansion into a short book
was recommended. The direct relevance of this topic to the New
Orleans 1987 General Congress on the Holy Spirit and World
Evangelism was a major stimulus in the decision to accept this
recommendation.

The preparation of this book in time for the New Orleans
Congress in July 1987 has influenced two major changes in perspective from the Sedalia paper. First, whereas the Sedalia paper
was prepared for a Catholic audience, this book treats the same
questions, but in a way that is not primarily geared to a Catholic
public. It therefore addresses the issues concerning the renewal
in the Holy Spirit and the unity of the church in a way that
concerns all Christians of whatever tradition. Secondly, the
Sedalia paper was for a more specialist audience, and was accompanied by a generous serving of footnotes. This book, while
dealing with serious issues involving important theological principles, is addressed to a wider public. It is hoped that it will reach
and be appreciated by any Christians concerned with the Lord's
purpose in this outpouring of the Holy Spirit.

The first part of the book examines the charismatic movement
(the renewal in the Holy Spirit, the neo-Pentecostal movement),
first to see what it is and what characterizes it; secondly, to seek
to understand its meaning. Only then can any of us be in a position
to consider the relationship between this movement and the
Christian churches. To the author's knowledge, this has not been
attempted before in this way.

I have dedicated this book in gratitude for the life and work of two great Pentecostal men of unity, Thomas Roberts and David du Plessis. David du Plessis has been much the better known among English-speaking Christians, and so it is unnecessary here to detail his distinctive contribution to this topic. However, it is worth noting that David du Plessis more than any other person held together the Pentecostal and the charismatic movements. He did this when there were powerful pressures on both sides to keep the other movement at a distance. By his witness to the baptism in the Holy Spirit as the heart of both movements, David du Plessis made clear their God-given affinity and the corresponding divine call that both accept this unity in the Spirit.

Thomas Roberts was a Welshman, who spent almost all his adult life in France. Born in 1902, he was brought up in the aftermath of the Welsh revival of 1904-06. Formed in the Apostolic Church, a new Pentecostal denomination of Welsh origin, Thomas Roberts was sent to France in 1926 as a missionary on the basis of a prophecy. Though he later left the Apostolics, disturbed by their refusal to recognize the Lord's work in other Protestant Christians, he always retained his pentecostal witness as the minister of an independent Reformed church. In World War II, when he could have taken his family back to Britain before the Nazi occupation, he chose to remain and be interned, so as to share the suffering of the French people with whom the Lord had identified him. After the war, Thomas Roberts was closely associated with the Union de Prière, a group of Reformed ministers first touched by the Pentecostal movement in the South of France in the 1930s. This was a kind of ecumenical charismatic group before its time. The Union de Prière focused on prayer for four intentions: the revival of the churches by the conversion of souls; the salvation of the Jewish people; the visible unity of the body of Christ; and the Second Coming of Jesus Christ and the resurrection of the dead. What the Lord taught Thomas Roberts through his participation in the Union de Prière was a preparation for the last twenty years of his life. This final phase, the crown of his life and ministry, began when he heard of the outpouring of the Holy Spirit on Episcopalians and others in the United States in the early 1960s. He was deeply stirred by this news. Seven years later he was thrilled by the news of the spread of this movement to the Roman Catholic Church. During these years, Thomas Roberts grew in his grasp of the vision of one reunited body of Christ, manifesting the glory of the Savior and the power of his Spirit to the world. He grew in his understanding of how the people of Israel are included in this mystery of the wedding of the Lamb. Roberts was a model of a Christian who always remained faithful to his original call—he was always characteristically Pentecostal—yet who was so grateful to the Lord for opening his eyes to see the riches of other Christian traditions, Protestant, Catholic and Orthodox. Thomas Roberts was the man who had the vision for a European congress of Christians united in the Holy Spirit, a vision which took shape and was realized in the "Pentecost over Europe" celebration at Strasbourg, France in 1982. His next vision was for Christians to be brought together in Jerusalem, in 1984, but before a modified version of his vision could be realized, he was called home by the Lord in December, 1983.

This book is dedicated to the Lord in gratitude for these two Pentecostal pioneers. This is because the renewal in the Holy Spirit would hardly have been possible without the Pentecostal movement. And neither the Pentecostal movement nor the charismatic movement can realize its God-given potential without the other. David du Plessis and Thomas Roberts knew this, and they lived it. Praise God for their example. May we follow it!

Peter Hocken
Mother of God Community
Gaithersburg, Maryland
March 1987

In gratitude to God for the
memory of two great
Pentecostal men of unity
Thomas Roberts
and
David du Plessis

Part I

WHAT IS THIS RENEWAL IN THE HOLY SPIRIT?

CHAPTER ONE

Stories of the Living God

THE CHARISMATIC MOVEMENT IS A MOVEMENT OF THE HOLY Spirit of God, deeply touching and transforming the lives of people. It is a movement bringing the vivid revitalizing experience of God our Father and his Son, our Lord Jesus Christ. In its beginnings, it spread primarily by word of mouth, as excited Christians hastened to share with family, friends and others what God had done for them in the baptism in the Holy Spirit. In other words, this movement began to grow as the apostolic church grew after the day of Pentecost.

This book seeks to probe more deeply the meaning of this outpouring. We cannot do better than to start with the testimonies of believers baptized in the Holy Spirit. No amount of scholarly studies on its meaning can replace the basic witness of those who have seen, who have looked upon and who have touched in some way the reality of the risen Lord. As you read these witnesses, allow the Holy Spirit to reveal to you the wonder of what is being described. Ask the divine comforter to show you the heart of this life-giving work. This will help you to see the full significance of this act of God, that will be examined in the following chapters.

Tommy Tyson, Methodist minister, North Carolina (1950)

One Sunday Morning the Sunday School lesson was based on the second chapter of Acts. I attended the adult men's class that morning. Most of the men were members of the Official Board of the Church. When the teacher finished the lesson, he turned to me and asked if I had anything to offer. Something within suggested that I get up in front of all these men whom I served as pastor and tell them about my great need and desire for the experience described in Acts 2. I thought to myself "if I tell these men all about my need and searching desire, they will think I am foolish and will lose confidence in me. If this happens, I thought, I'll no longer have a ministry here." This inward voice seemed to say, "Well, do you want a ministry or do you want to be baptized in The Holy Ghost?" I got to my feet and came around to the lectern with the full conviction that this meant the end of all my personal desires and dreams in terms of being a successful pastor. I began to make a full confession before these men. I told them how I had feared their opinion, how I had courted their favor and how God had put such a hunger in my heart to be filled with his Spirit. Heaven began to break through. Fear and inhibitions began to depart. Holy Joy and Holy Love began to flood my mind and spirit and body. This high ecstasy continued through the morning worship service. Ignoring my prepared sermon, I came down in front of the chancel and just talked about the Love of Jesus. His Love was being poured out through me in great joy.

Following the service, the entire afternoon was spent in spontaneous praise and thanksgiving. I had prayed before but never like this. Most of my prayer had been petition for self and others or times of meditation and quiet listening. Without an awareness of time, the afternoon was gone and evening service time had come. The evening service was a continuation of the same. After the service, some of the members invited me and others to their home for further prayer. . . .

There were about twenty or thirty people present, most of whom were members of the Church which I pastored. I did not know what was happening to me but I was trying to give the loved ones there a description. I was more aware of Heaven than I was of earth and as I sought to describe something of what I saw in the heavenly world, the words were foreign to me. The language being used was not English. Other gifts of The Holy Spirit were made manifest, including the Gift of Knowledge, The Gift of

Prophecy, and the Gift of The Discernment of Spirits. The entire world was given new meaning. It even looked different. There is a rare beauty about all God's creation when seen through the eyes of Heaven.

Edgar Trout, Methodist lay preacher, Plymouth, England (1958)

One evening at Bath Street early in 1958 a woman handed him a grubby piece of paper on which was written the message. "Come to this address next Thursday evening, Mr. Trout, and you'll get a blessing from the Lord." Dismissing the lady in his mind as a "poor old soul" he carried on with his business. Later that evening however he was convicted in conscience about his treatment of the woman. He felt God telling him:

> Tonight you treated one of My children as if she did not count, as if she did not exist. Who are you to judge, just because she appeared to you a bit eccentric? I sent her. She was My messenger to you.

Trout obeyed the unknown messenger. He went to the hall, even though in the meantime he had discovered that it was the meeting-place of a rowdy Pentecostal group known as the "Gloryland" Assembly. His first impressions confirmed his worst fears of unbridled emotionalism, exhibitionism and superficiality. Only when a small elderly lady began singing in a strange language did Trout sense a reverence and something of God's peace. When the pastor issued an altar call, Trout felt no inclination to respond. But he was astonished to see his staid Anglican companion leave his seat. With somewhat mixed feelings he followed suit. When the pastor came to pray for Trout, the extraordinary happened:

> For in the next instant he was suddenly overwhelmed, and well nigh knocked off his knees, by an almost unbearable consciousness of the presence of God. It was as if he had been transported, in the twinkling of an eye, to the purest

5

realms of everlasting light, and was kneeling right before the very Throne of the Father. All he could do was weakly bow his head in awe and worship, as light and love broke over him. At first he was too choked to speak. What he was experiencing, within himself and without, was too deep and holy, too immeasurably vast, too intensely real, for shallow, shadowy words to express. . . . Then all at once his whole being let out its love and adoration in an ecstatic gush of sound. They were words indeed that were pouring from him, but words in a language he had never before heard and could not for the life of him understand. He only knew that his spirit was communing with God in a way more direct, more fundamental, more basic to his innermost nature, than he had ever thought possible.

William T. Sherwood, Episcopalian priest, Florida (1959)

I finally decided to attend a Healing Conference (Camp Farthest Out at Ardmore, Okla.) in the Fall of 1959. My good luck (God's tremendous grace) caused me to room with a brother priest, an Anglo-Catholic like myself, the Rev. Wilbur Fogg, then of Decatur, Ill. Through him, just before the inspiring seven day Conference ended, I found the glorious experience which I can only think of as "THE GIFT." It was the very experience of the one hundred and twenty at Pentecost; of the "only baptized" people to whom Peter and John came in Samaria; of the Gentiles in the home of Cornelius; of the ones at Ephesus upon whom St. Paul laid hands—after baptizing them in the Name of Jesus. For like them, I found myself, to my own utter amazement, baptized "with the Holy Ghost and with fire" and speaking in an entirely unknown language—words that I knew deep in my heart were praises to the Saviour God, whom for three years I had been putting in second place in my easy-going, hobby-filled life! At last, in the little prayer meeting Fr. Fogg had taken me to, I was giving my heart to Jesus in utter and complete abandon; I was loving

Him as I NEVER had loved Him before. I knew now at long last that "He was mine, and I was His, forever!"

I had known periods of surrendered life before. Back in the early days of the Oxford Group I had known what it was to be truly guided, and to sing in my heart to the Lord, as I went about His work. But this was on a deeper level, and brought a greater sense of security and joy in Him than ANYTHING I had ever known.

I returned to my work a new man. I felt, and people told me I looked, twenty years younger. Two weeks later I became seventy and I felt younger, happier and stronger, than I had at fifty. God was so good! And the new joy, thanks be to Him, was contagious. The semi-defunct prayer group came alive. Souls were saved; people were healed. For weeks I walked in an ecstasy of bliss that words cannot describe. God had baptized me with the Holy Ghost, in a way that I SHOULD have been baptized at Confirmation—but, not expecting it then, how COULD I be!

Dennis Bennett, Episcopalian priest, California (1959)

We sat down on opposite sides of the room and began to pray. Again there was no attempt to "work me up," no emotionalism or excitement. Once more I prayed very quietly and cautiously, and this time, after only about three or four minutes, words began to come in another language, the same language, I noted, that I had spoken on the previous Saturday—at least it sounded like it. Again, I was in no way compelled to speak this new tongue. It was something that I could do if I chose. I was in no strange state of mind whatsoever, and was in full possession of whatever wits I normally had! The dynamics of the new language were entirely under my control: whether I spoke or not, whether I spoke loudly or softly, fast or slow, high or low. The only thing that was not under my volition was the form of the words and sounds that came when I chose to let them come. After all, how could I formulate words in a language I didn't know? . . .

I still felt nothing out of the ordinary: no great spiritual inspiration, no special inner warmth of God's presence. It was interesting, though, and somehow refreshing, and so I spoke on for several minutes. I was about to stop, but John said:

"Don't stop. Go on. Go on speaking."

It proved to be good advice. I went on, allowing the new words to come to my lips, and after three or four more minutes began to sense something new. This language was being given me from the central place in me where God was, far beyond the realm of my emotions. Speaking on and on, I became more and more aware of God in me. The words didn't mean anything to me as language, but God knew exactly what they meant. God living in me was creating the language. I was speaking it—giving it voice, by my volition, and I was speaking it to God Who was above and beyond me. God the Holy Spirit was giving me the words to talk to God the Father, and it was all happening because of God the Son, Jesus Christ. As I spoke I had a vivid mental picture of Jesus on the Cross.

Judy Yates, Baptist, Santa Barbara, California (1961)

In February, 1961, I received a phone call from Dr. Frost stating that someone named Jean Stone was visiting in their home and would tell of the way God was moving in Los Angeles. He added the Spirit was moving in the same real way right here in Santa Barbara. He invited me to come and meet Mrs. Stone. I knew that this might be the thing I had been looking for. I opened my heart before the Lord and told him that if this was of Him, I wanted it.

That afternoon I heard things that could have come out of the Book of Acts itself, but these things were happening today, not 2,000 years ago. I heard how the Lord was healing people—people with real (and in some instances incurable infirmities), not

8

just imaginary ills. I heard how the Holy Spirit was speaking to and through the people, not in a natural, normal way, but in a supernatural language. These people were not in some small, unheard-of sect, but were Episcopalians, Methodists, Presbyterians and, believe it or not, even Baptists! I had been a Christian for six years, and for all these six years had attended a Baptist Church, but never had I heard of things like this. I was almost afraid to believe all I heard, yet I knew that every word was true.

As Mrs. Stone spoke, I again prayed that if this was of God, then I wanted to speak in an unknown tongue also. If it was not of God, I wanted no part of it. After talking a little more and asking a few questions, I was asked if I wanted to be prayed for that I might enter into this same experience. For just a split second I was afraid, but then the Lord assured me that this was for me and was from Him. We prayed, and just as with the others I had heard about that day, the Holy Spirit gave me a new language of prayer and praise. Just as was my initial conversion experience, this experience was quiet and gentle, but very real.

The two years that have followed that initial experience have not all been perfect. There have been times in my life that I have not listened to the promptings of the Holy Spirit. There have been times that I have quenched His leading. As I have confessed these times to Him I have found that He is willing to make His presence again real in my life. Through these experiences in the Holy Spirit I have found that Jesus is always the focal point. He is the One to Whom the Holy Spirit points. I am learning that there are depths in the Lord Jesus that I have not yet begun to explore. I have also found that because of this reality of Jesus Christ I have not again doubted this continued experience with the Holy Spirit. I am learning in a far deeper way who Jesus is.

Larry Christenson, Lutheran pastor, California (1961)

An elderly Norwegian lady—formerly a member of the Hauge Lutheran Synod, now a member of the Foursquare Gospel

Church in San Pedro—called me up one day and asked if she might invite some of our people to a revival they were having. As it turned out, I was the one she was inviting. I had a free evening the following Thursday and decided it would be good relaxation to hear somebody else preach for a change!

The evangelist, Mary Westberg, was speaking on the gifts of the Spirit, out of 1 Corinthians 12. The Lord spoke to me in that sermon. I went up to her afterward, thanked her for the message, and said I would appreciate her prayers: I wanted a more Spirit-filled ministry. She asked if I had received the "baptism." I gave her a puzzled look. "The baptism with the Holy Spirit," she explained. "Well, I don't know." I answered, a little uncertainly, "not as a definite experience, at any rate." This was unfamiliar terminology to me.

She and her husband offered to pray with me. They said that I should simply yield my tongue to the Lord and he would give me a new language—an "unknown tongue"—with which to praise Him. My mind was racing with a thousand questions, doubts, uncertainties, fears. Overriding all else was the fear of "faking" anything—of letting my desire for a blessing from the Lord run out ahead of his Spirit. They prayed and I prayed, but nothing demonstrable happened.

That night, sometime after midnight, I woke from a light sleep, sat bolt-upright in bed, and found an "unknown tongue" hovering on my lips. Fully aware of what I was doing, I spoke a sentence in the tongue—and promptly fell back to sleep. I woke up in the morning with a clear recollection of the experience, though at first I thought I might only have dreamed it. Later in the week, however, I experienced this new kind of prayer when I was fully awake. It has been a valuable part of my prayer life ever since.

That is how it began with me—an interest in healing and the experience of speaking in tongues.

These initial events were a kind of doorway into a new dimension of spiritual awareness. Since then I have known the reality of

Christ in a new way. Before, it was primarily my thoughts that were affected, my system of ideas. Now it is my life and actions, and my deeper attitudes and feelings as well. Faith has taken on a more personal quality. Prayer has become a cornerstone of daily life. The Word of God has gained a new power to shape my thought and action. I have come into more deeply committed relationships with other Christians. Concern for the upbuilding of the church, and for her witness in the world, is not simply an ideal, nor a task; it is a daily conversation with the Lord of the Church. All of this I attribute to the work of the Spirit.

Brian Casebow, Church of Scotland minister, Edinburgh, Scotland (1962)

Round about this time too a friend, Gordon, studying divinity at Edinburgh wrote me an enthusiastic letter about a group that were beginning to pray for a deeper knowledge of the Holy Spirit as a real power that works. I suddenly realised that for me the Holy Spirit was just the third person of a theological concept. I didn't know him as I knew the Father and the Son. . . .

When Gordon went back to Edinburgh that day, I went to my Bible, to Luke's gospel in particular, and went through it carefully considering every word of Jesus to see what it all meant. I recommend this to anyone who is in doubt. From that moment I was convinced and began to pray eagerly and sincerely for the Spirit.

Almost at once my life was rewarded by a new sense of purpose, of being under the guidance of my Lord Himself. The word of God became the Word of God, absolutely, nothing less. Each day became an adventure for Him. The very colours of the world around me seemed brighter and fresher. I began to *preach* again—that is, I began to glorify my crucified Saviour, alive and risen for ever. How I praised Him and longed to know the fullness of his glory!

11

During the next months I grew in faith. I was reading *Trinity Magazine* very closely and eagerly, also reading the amazing stories of people like Oral Roberts, Agnes Sanford, Elsie Salmon, and so many others. I began to long for the gift of healing.

On May the 27th, a Sunday evening, after the evening service I was reading *Trinity* in my study quite alone when on a sudden impulse I went down on my knees and immediately the experience was mine. What else can we call it except the Baptism of the Holy Spirit promised by John the Baptist, received at the hand of Jesus our Lord.

I had tried to speak in tongues before. No use. It cannot be imitated. Now suddenly I was gushing forth strange words and almost weeping with the joy of His presence.

I don't think the experience lasted long. The power died away and I began to doubt. Two friends told me the following week, although they had not had the experience themselves, "When you have it you will be quite sure." I wasn't sure, but then it must be remembered that up until this time I had never heard the phenomena! In fact I first heard tongues spoken by someone else when Gordon returned from England a week later—baptized himself!

I had a miserable week doubting it. I caught a horrid cold which depressed me a great deal. However the following Wednesday I received the go-ahead from God to form a group of minister friends to discuss the whole issue. I prayed to see who should be invited. Tongues came to my lips, then came doubts, but I pushed them aside with an almost physical sensation to meet another physical sensation—the sensation that I was seeing the cross itself, the cross of my dear Saviour. Every doubt vanished from that moment.

Patricia Gallagher Mansfield, Catholic, Duquesne (1967)

The next day we started discussing the chapters in Acts. One of the professors told us that the reason Catholics don't experience the power of the Holy Spirit is because they don't have the faith to expect great things from God. Just as we must constantly reaffirm what happened to us at baptism, we need a greater openness to the Spirit of God as we grow and mature. He warned us that God listens and answers our prayers and asked if we were ready for what God would do for us. I honestly admitted I was scared, and yet I tacked up a note on the bulletin board which read, "I want a miracle." Some of us agreed to ask the chaplain if, as part of the closing ceremony of Sunday, we could have a renewal of confirmation vows.

In the meantime, the Lord had other plans for us. That night we had scheduled a party, but nobody seemed to be ready for light talking or dancing. I wandered up to the chapel without really knowing why, but as soon as I knelt down I began to tremble. Suddenly I didn't want to leave. I remember reasoning with myself that Christ is in other people and that I should go down with them and not expect to spend my whole life in a chapel. There were three other students with me when all of a sudden I became filled with the Holy Spirit and realized that "God is real." I started laughing and crying at the same time, because not only did I know that he is real, but that he loves us. And this love that he has is almost foolish because we're so unworthy and yet he continues to freely give us his grace. I wanted to share this wonderful knowledge and joy with the others, but they seemed so detached. For a moment I thought it might just be a beautiful dream. The next thing I knew I was prostrate before the altar and filled with the peace of Christ.

I experienced what it means "to dwell in his love." In coming home to the Father who made me I felt more complete and free than ever before. I knew I was unworthy and did not have enough faith, and yet I was begging him to stay and never leave me. As much as I wanted to remain there with him I knew, just as the apostles after Pentecost, that I must share this with others. If I could experience the love and power of God in this way, anyone could. That night the Lord brought the whole group into the chapel. I found my prayers pouring forth that the others might come to know him, too. My former shyness about praying aloud was completely gone as the Holy Spirit spoke through me. The professors then laid hands on some of the students, but most of us received the "baptism in the Spirit" while kneeling before the blessed sacrament in prayer. Some of us started speaking in tongues, others received gifts of discernment, prophecy, and wisdom. But the most important gift was the fruit of love which bound the whole community together. In the Lord's Spirit we found a unity we had long tried to achieve on our own.

Chapter Two

How Did All This Begin?

"PENTECOST HAS COME." IN 1906, THIS STARTLING MESSAGE went out from as unexpected a source as Nazareth in Galilee: a ramshackle wooden building in a poor section of Los Angeles. The message was startling because this chapel in Azusa Street was not simply witnessing the power of God in revival, but was seeing the same wondrous gifts of the Holy Spirit as were manifest on the day of Pentecost. Speaking in other tongues, prophecy, healing, all were occurring in the midst of an explosion of spontaneous praise of Almighty God and Our Lord Jesus Christ. By September of that year, visitors were beginning to flock to Azusa Street from far and near, pastors, missionaries on furlough, ordinary believers, some earnest seekers for a deeper life with the Lord, some curious, some sceptical. Few were untouched by what they saw.

Reminiscent too of the first Pentecost was the diversity of those who came. In an America still nursing the wounds of the Civil War with its deep rift over race and slavery, it was a powerful sign in itself that Azusa Street was led by a black pastor from Louisiana, William J. Seymour, then aged about thirty-four. It was an astonishing sight, the mixture of black, white and oriental, of well-to-do and desperately poor, of educated and uneducated, pushing forward to receive together the same blessing of God, the baptism in the Holy Spirit.

The word from Azusa Street found its most receptive soil in those groups of Christians who had been excited by hearing of the revival in Wales that began in late 1904. Whole towns and villages in Wales were being visited by the Lord; thousands and thousands of people, many hardened in the ways of sin, were being reconciled to God; chapels were being filled daily by expectant and enthusiastic throngs desiring to praise God and to be refreshed by his Spirit. This news inspired zealous and prayerful believers in other lands to beg the Lord to pour out his new life in their own midst. Many of these expectant Christians saw Azusa Street as God's answer to their prayers. The ground was prepared for this message of Pentecost to speed around the world.

It was astonishing how rapidly this happened. At the end of 1906, the impetus from Azusa Street was boosted by a campaign of Charles Parham in Zion City, Illinois, which brought many new apostles into the burgeoning Pentecostal movement. By 1908, the message had reached every major city in the United States. Also by this time, missionaries from Azusa Street had taken this word of power to China, to India, and to West and South Africa. In India, the new Pentecostal drive gained added thrust from the spontaneous revival that had broken out among the child widows at Pandita Ramabai's homes near Poona.

The message reached Europe even sooner. A Methodist minister from Norway, T. B. Barratt, on an unsuccessful fund-raising trip to the United States, found that God had something much better in store. He heard of the outpouring at Azusa Street, and was himself baptized in the Spirit in late 1906 in New York City. Taking the message of Pentecost back to his church in Oslo, Barratt unexpectedly found himself the major catalyst for this new movement in Europe. Visitors from England and Germany took back the reports of this Pentecost to their own countries. All Saints church in Sunderland, a rather bleak city in the north-east of England, then became a kind of mini-Azusa Street, where many came to receive the baptism in the Spirit. These included a largely illiterate plumber from Bradford, Yorkshire, whose name was Smith Wigglesworth.

Who were the people who heard and received this message, the people we have come to call the Pentecostals? In the United States, the majority had been Christians involved in some way in the Holiness movement, people who believed in and desired a life of sanctification, a life in which decisive victory over sin was experienced. In other parts of the world, the movement caused a stir in many evangelical Protestant circles, especially on many of the mission stations. It did not seem to impinge on the world of the major Protestant denominations, except perhaps in Germany, where the gifts of the Spirit were the subject of fierce debate and a group of theologians and pastors denounced the Pentecostal movement as a devilish invention from "below." In England, however, the major figure at the start of the movement was an Anglican priest, Alexander A. Boddy, who was strongly supported by another Anglican, Cecil H. Polhill, a former missionary to China.

Leaders like Boddy and Polhill in Britain, and Jonathan Paul in Germany, were not successful in rallying their churches to this movement of Pentecost. Within a few years, the vast majority of those baptized in the Spirit "with signs following" had become members of new Pentecostal denominations. Some of these groups were small Holiness denominations that became Pentecostal almost *en bloc*, though the larger part was made up of new groupings gathering together many of the new independent congregations. This was true of the American Assemblies of God (1915), the Pentecostal Assemblies of Canada (1919) and the British Assemblies of God (1925).

So within twenty years of the Azusa Street outbreak, the new life of baptism in the Spirit with the spiritual gifts was almost wholly restricted to the Pentecostal churches, many of them subdividing through doctrinal conflict and clashing personalities. The historic churches, Protestant, Orthodox and Catholic, continued in almost total ignorance of what had happened at Azusa Street.

It was in this situation that in 1936 Smith Wigglesworth, during a trip to South Africa, gave a prophecy that is perhaps the most significant prophetic word in the history of the Pentecostal movement. One morning, Wigglesworth strode into a Pentecostal church office in Johannesburg, where he pinned a young church official to the wall and began to prophesy. This young man, David du Plessis, recalled the shock of Wigglesworth's words:

> There is a revival coming that at present the world knows nothing about. It will come through the churches. It will come in a fresh way. When you see what God does in this revival you will then have to admit that all that you have seen previously is a mere nothing in comparison with what is to come. It will eclipse anything that has been known in history. Empty churches, empty cathedrals, will be packed again with worshippers. Buildings will not be able to accommodate the multitudes. Then you will see fields of people worshipping and praising together. The Lord intends to use you in this revival. For you have been in Jerusalem long enough. The Lord will send you to the uttermost parts of the earth. If you are faithful and humble, the Lord will use you and if you remain faithful and humble, you will see the greatest events in church history.

Neither Wigglesworth nor du Plessis previously thought that the Holy Spirit could anoint and penetrate the historic churches. Du Plessis often told the story of how he remonstrated with the Lord, "But, Lord, these churches are dead." But he got the response, "I am the One who raises the dead." Wigglesworth's prophecy shows God's longing to renew the face of the earth, and to touch the whole world. Marvelous as the work of the Pentecostals has been, especially in their evangelizing millions of the lost, the movement of Azusa Street that united black and white so remarkably in Christ was meant to do more than create a cluster of dynamic new denominations. Now in this prophecy, du Plessis heard that God had not given up on the old churches, just as he never gave up on his covenant people in the Old Testament, however far they strayed from his ways. The new move, prophesied by Wigglesworth, was to be a second chance.

Wigglesworth told du Plessis that this new outpouring would not begin until after his own death. Wigglesworth died in 1947, and in the following year, du Plessis was injured in a serious accident at a railroad crossing in West Virginia. During his convalescence, he heard an inner voice saying: "The time for the prophecy Smith Wigglesworth gave you has arrived. It is time to begin. I want you to go to the leaders of the churches." This was the beginning of the extraordinary ecumenical witness of the man who came to be known as "Mr. Pentecost." First, he went to the offices of the World Council of Churches in New York City, and through the 1950s, he received an increasing number of invitations to major church gatherings, some denominational, some ecumenical. Wherever he went, he bore witness to Jesus as the baptizer in the Holy Spirit.

Even before Wigglesworth's death, a handful of Protestant Christians had received the baptism in the Spirit with the sign of tongues without leaving their churches. This was true of Louis Dallière, a Reformed pastor in France, who was convicted by the preaching of a Pentecostal evangelist and received "the baptism" early in the 1930s, out of which grew a small movement in which the gifts of the Spirit were exercised. In West Germany, a small new Protestant religious congregation, the Mary Sisters, led by Basilea Schlink, experienced gifts of the Spirit as they surrendered to the Lord in the devastated surroundings of Darmstadt at the end of World War II. It was also true of Harald Bredesen, a Dutch Reformed pastor in New York City, who received the baptism in the Spirit at a Pentecostal camp meeting in 1946.

The number of Protestant Christians being touched by God in this way grew steadily throughout the 1950s without attracting much attention. Many men, including some ministers, came into this blessing through the activities of the Full Gospel Business

Men's Fellowship International, founded in the early 1950s by a dairy millionaire, Demos Shakarian, whose story has been told in *The Happiest People on Earth*. FGBMFI spread rapidly across the American continent and then overseas, bringing the message of the pentecostal baptism at prayer breakfasts and conventions to people who would not go near a Pentecostal church. In Holland, some young theological students from the Dutch Reformed Church were baptized in the Spirit around 1952, after seeing the power of God in healing, and this led to the publication of one of the first charismatic magazines *Vuur* (Fire). An American Episcopalian, Agnes Sanford, already well-known for her healing ministry through her book *The Healing Light*, was led into the pentecostal baptism around 1954-55, and immediately began telling others of it privately and in counseling situations. This ministry was a major reason why the movement in the United States, when it became more public, involved so many Episcopalian priests. In Britain, several intercessors in the London Healing Mission began praying in tongues around 1957-58.

Prayer groups that would later be called charismatic sprang up in several places in the late 1950s: for example, in Trinity Episcopal Church at Wheaton, Illinois (under Richard Winkler), in Upper Octorara Presbyterian Church, Parkesburg, Pennsylvania (under James Brown) and in Mount Vernon Dutch Reformed Church, New York City (under Harald Bredesen). Meanwhile the Vuur movement in Holland had its numbers swelled by the campaign of Pentecostal evangelist, T.L. Osborn, in 1958. 1959 saw the beginning of the prayer group that met in the home of Edgar Trout, the Methodist lay preacher and businessman in Plymouth, England, whose witness was given in Chapter One.

So when Dennis Bennett announced to a startled congregation at St. Mark's, Van Nuys, California in April 1960 that he had been filled with the Spirit and was speaking in other tongues, a new phase of this work of God was beginning because the resulting furore gave the movement its first national publicity in *Newsweek* and *Time* magazines. Although Bennett immediately resigned from the pastorate, members of the Van Nuys prayer group led by Jean Stone formed the Blessed Trinity Society, which from 1961-66 produced a quarterly magazine called *Trinity*. Each issue was filled with witnesses of people in the mainline churches who had been baptized in the Spirit. These included many ministers and priests, including a number of Episcopalians of high church and sacramental leanings. This was perhaps the first sign that this new move was to reach out beyond the circles of evangelical Christians to become a truly ecumenical movement, touching Christians in all the historic church traditions.

In 1961, Larry Christenson, pastor of Trinity Lutheran Church, San Pedro, California received, and his church gradually became a focal point for charismatic renewal among Lutherans. Dennis Bennett's new parish, St. Mark's in Seattle, also became a center of renewal in the Spirit, where many, including individual Roman Catholics, came, first to enquire and then to receive. Harald Bredesen was invited to speak at Yale, and the resulting clamor over Yale students speaking in tongues received much publicity. By 1963, most attentive Christians in the United States were aware that something new was stirring in the land! In that year, at least ten major Protestant church journals published articles on "glossolalia," as speaking in tongues was called by the more learned.

Meanwhile, the movement was becoming visible in other countries. By early 1963, quite a number of individual Christians in the major Protestant churches of Great Britain had received "the baptism." It became more public with visits to Britain in 1963 by Frank Maguire, by Larry Christenson and by David du Plessis. Michael Harper, a young Anglican priest in London, who had experienced a deep purification and cleansing the previous fall, became the main organizer of the meetings, at which the visitors from the U.S. spoke and witnessed. Many clergy attended these gatherings, and the new movement began to attract attention in the church press. The same European trip of Larry Christenson also led to Arnold Bittlinger, a young Lutheran pastor, receiving and that began a movement in the German Evangelical Lutheran Church.

Throughout the mid-1960s, this movement of the Spirit was gaining momentum. Not only Episcopalians, Lutherans and Presbyterians were being touched, but also Baptists, Methodists, Mennonites and members of small Protestant churches. But early in 1967, God sprang another great surprise, perhaps as big as any in this whole story. The Holy Spirit was poured out with his gifts on a group of Roman Catholics, first at a retreat week-end near Pittsburgh, and soon after at gatherings in South Bend, Indiana and East Lansing, Michigan.

Only those Christians with a knowledge of how deeply the Protestant world has suspected and opposed the Roman Catholic Church can sense what a bombshell this was, especially when the Catholics concerned quickly showed that they had no intention of leaving their church. Indeed, they saw this coming of the Spirit of God as a direct answer to Pope John XXIII's call at the Second Vatican Council for the Holy Spirit to come upon the church as at a "new Pentecost." Here, they felt, was a divine answer to all the Catholic prayers for renewal of the church.

The charismatic renewal among Catholics began in a significantly different way from its origins among Protestants. It began among young people, it began among lay people, and it began in university settings. Each of these points is significant. For in a church, indeed the largest church in Christendom, led—some critics would say dominated—by clergy and often elderly clergy, this move of the Spirit began among the young and among those who had no intention of entering the ordained ministry. Also for a movement that had often been seen as anti-intellectual, opposing the enthusiasm of the heart to the calculations of the mind, it was bursting out among young people of high intellectual calibre. Another feature significant for the future was that these young

Catholics at Duquesne, South Bend and Michigan State were led by those who had known each other for years and had prayed and served together in Catholic student group activities on the Notre Dame campus during the later part of the Second Vatican Council. This is the main reason why so quickly after the visitation of early 1967, this Holy Spirit renewal among Catholics became organized beyond what had happened in any other church, and quickly gave rise to pastoral structures and tools, such as Life in the Spirit seminars, renewal conferences, *New Covenant* magazine and new forms of covenant community.

Around the same time as the movement broke out among Catholics, a few Orthodox Christians were also baptized in the Spirit. Some were students or recent graduates in the same circles as the newly-anointed young Catholics, but another was a priest, Fr. Athanasios Emmert.

Most of the English-speaking world had been reached by this visitation of the Holy Spirit by the end of the 1960s, and the movement continued to gather momentum through the 1970s. The 1970s also saw its rapid expansion in other parts of the world, from the early 1970s in Latin America, Scandinavia, France and Italy, from the mid-1970s in Spain, Portugal, Africa and Asia.

Virtually every church tradition in each continent has now been touched in some way by this pentecostal fire. The only churches in which it appears to be absent are those which have expelled their members who laid claim to this blessing. But even some of these—the Plymouth Brethren, the Church of the Nazarene, the Church of God (Anderson), Indiana—are more recently showing signs of moderating their opposition.

Thus, in his own divine order, God has reached down to touch members of all the different Christian traditions. We can speculate on why it has happened in the way that it has, indeed we can reverently seek his light on God's chosen means. We may guess with a high degree of certainty that it would have been impossible for the Roman Catholic Church to have accepted a movement that began among Protestants, before the historic decree on ecumenism passed at the Second Vatican Council in 1964. There, the Catholic bishops explicitly recognized the presence of the Holy Spirit working in other churches, a conviction of which they were soon to receive stronger evidence. But what is more important is to recognize that it has happened, and that it is a wonder in our eyes. We are truly a privileged people to witness this grace, to see people from all traditions and backgrounds together receiving what we had not thought possible. Both the *what* (the blessing given) and the *who* (the range of the recipients) exceed our past hopes and expectations. Of our generation, the words of Jesus can be said: "Blessed are your eyes, for they see, and your ears, for they hear. Truly, I say to you, many prophets and righteous men longed to see what you see, and did not see it, and to hear what you hear, and did not hear it" (Matthew 13:16-17).

CHAPTER THREE

New Life in Christ Jesus

WHAT IS IT THAT HAPPENED TO ALL THESE PEOPLE? WHAT actually happened to them when they were baptized in the Holy Spirit? Although each experience was personal, with details reflecting each recipient's individual history and present situation, what was most significant was common to all testimonies. Some had an overpowering experience, while others did not. Some were lost in praise for hours on end, while others had a quiet peace and weren't quite sure what had happened. But all knew either immediately or over a period that they were changed men and women, touched by the Spirit of God. It has been one of the most exciting aspects of this work of the Lord, when people from radically different church traditions have met and recognized in each other, "God has done the same thing in you that he has done in me." People baptized in the Spirit recognize a deep affinity with others who have received the same blessing.

What then are the central elements in this spiritual transformation called the baptism in the Spirit? At this stage, we will not try to sort out what is primary and what is secondary, what is cause and what is effect, but simply note the common elements found in the testimonies of people baptized in the Holy Spirit.

1. *Personal Encounter with Jesus.* The witnesses regularly show a new level of encounter with Jesus Christ, the risen Lord. Recipients have experienced the truth of Jesus' words about the work of the Holy Spirit, "he will take what is mine and declare it to you" (John 16:14). People know the reality of the Lord Jesus in a vivid way. They know his love, and his mercy. It is noteworthy how many witnesses speak of having some vision, image or revelation of the cross of Jesus. That is how the infinite love of the

Savior is known, not so much by feeling good or warm, but by the Lord himself unveiling the love of his heart that took him to the cross of Calvary.

Another common element is a new knowledge of the Lordship of Jesus. Probably the most common theme at charismatic conferences has been "Jesus is Lord." Christians baptized in the Spirit know inside themselves the truth of what Paul wrote to the Corinthians, "no one can say, 'Jesus is Lord' except by the Holy Spirit" (1 Corinthians 12:3). Only the inner illumination of the mind by the Holy Spirit can bring that spiritual certainty that Jesus Christ, the son of Mary, the Son of God, is truly the Lord exercising all authority in heaven and on earth, enthroned at the right hand of the Father in majesty and glory.

2. *The Trinity Makes Sense.* How many in their Christian lives have felt that the mystery of the Trinity is beyond all comprehension! Three in One and One in Three sounds like a mathematical conundrum, or simply a logical impossibility. It is no more clear that there are three persons in the Trinity than that there might be two or four. But with the baptism in the Spirit, the doctrine of the Trinity makes sense to people. They may not be able to give a lecture on it, but they know the movement of the Holy Spirit within them that reveals the reality of Jesus, the only-begotten Son who opens the way to the Father. The Spirit within points to the Son who has become visible who points to the invisible Father.

Part of the Trinity making sense is knowing what it is to be sons and daughters of God. At his baptism Jesus heard the voice of the Father saying, "You are my beloved Son, with whom I am well pleased" (Mark 1:11). Just so when people are baptized in the Spirit they know in some way that the Father is saying to them, "You too are my beloved son/daughter because you are in Jesus my Son. In you I am well pleased." Chosen by the Father, redeemed by his Son, and indwelt by the Holy Spirit, they know they "are being changed into his likeness from one degree of glory to another" (2 Corinthians 3:18).

3. *God Speaks to Us.* This is one of the clearest differences between people baptized in the Spirit and those who are not. Those baptized in the Spirit know that the Lord still speaks to his people, both individually and collectively. This is an aspect of discovering God as our Father in heaven. For our heavenly Father does not communicate with his children less than the most loving human parent. This is part of what Jesus had in mind when he said, "If you then, who are evil, know how to give good gifts to your children, how much more will the heavenly Father give the Holy Spirit to those who ask him" (Luke 11:13). Charismatic testimonies regularly point to people beginning to hear the Lord! How often they say, "I never realized before that I could hear the living God speak to me." Those who have not had this experience are often alarmed by the claim that God speaks to his children today, and may make fun of people who think they have a "hot-line" to God. The less mocking and cynical may stress the need for discernment so that Christians do not uncritically accept every inner word or sense as being from the Holy Spirit. But the truth is that it is when people are baptized in the Spirit that discernment becomes highly relevant. Before that, there may not be much to discern!

Is there a regular pattern in charismatic testimonies as to what God says to his children? Yes, there is, and it goes back to the first point already made. What God speaks to his children most consistently is precisely what he said two thousand years ago, "In many and various ways God spoke of old to our fathers by the prophets; but in these last days he has spoken to us by a Son, whom he appointed the heir of all things" (Hebrews 1:1-2). What the Father tells his children is the glory of his Son, Jesus; the meaning of the blood of Jesus, shed for our sins; the meaning of his cross, by which he despoiled Satan, the ruler of this world; his plan to gather a people under the Lordship of Jesus, forming one united body that will glorify the Father; that Jesus will come again.

4. *The Ability to Praise God.* This is one of the most obvious signs of baptism in the Spirit to others present at the time. In the Scriptures, there is a verse, used by some churches in their liturgy, "O Lord, open my lips, and my mouth shall show forth your praise" (Psalm 51:15). When people are baptized in the Spirit, their mouths are opened. They do not need a prayer-book or a hymnal in order to open their mouths before God. By the Holy Spirit within, they are enabled to utter the praises of God. This new ability has several facets:

☐ This expression of the praise of God comes from a deeper level in the baptized person: it verifies the words of Jesus, "He who believes in me, as the scripture has said, 'Out of his heart shall flow rivers of living water'" (John 7:38). Whereas previous worship has come more out of the mind, somehow beginning and ending in the head, this praise in the Spirit flows from the very center of a person's being. Praise is not primarily the manifestation of an emotional state, but expresses the deepest spiritual convictions of the believer.

☐ What they are able to express far exceeds what they were able to express before. This is the deeper response to the revelation of the Spirit. As the Spirit reveals the majesty of Jesus to the inner spirit, so the spirit within is able to respond by worshipping the Lord who has revealed himself.

☐ The gift of praise includes a new degree of creativity: the person who so receives the Holy Spirit can speak spontaneously, alone and with others, of the Lord who has graciously declared himself. Even people who could never speak in public through nervousness or educational shortcomings find themselves able to declare the praises of God in their own words simply and without fear. We are reminded of Jesus' words of reproach to the chief priests and scribes when they criticized the spontaneous acclamations of the children, "Have you never read, 'Out of the mouth of babes and sucklings you have brought perfect praise?'" (Matthew 21:16).

5. *The Power to Evangelize.* This work of the Spirit has spread most through ordinary people telling others of their baptism in the Spirit and what the Lord has done for them. Once again there are several facets to this new ability to evangelize:

☐ There is an inner desire to tell others the good news. Beforehand, people may have known that Christians ought to proclaim the gospel of salvation, but they have lacked an inner drive to do so. Now with the Spirit penetrating the heart of their being, the love of God for lost humanity is within them. They begin to experience the urge of the Savior to risk rejection in order to reach all who do not know the salvation of God.

☐ They have something to say. They know within themselves the truth of the gospel, that Jesus died for their sins, and rose again that they might have life. They know this life is theirs, within them. And so they can speak of it. The man in John 9 declares, "one thing I know, that though I was blind, now I see" (John 9:25) and the apostles announce, "we cannot but speak of what we have seen and heard" (Acts 4:20). They can speak both of what they know of Jesus, and of what they know he has done for them.

☐ What they say now has a power to touch others that their best words before simply did not have. Because God's Spirit has now penetrated the heart, the believer can now speak words from the heart that are anointed by the Spirit of God and have the power to pierce the hearts of others. It is only the Word of God that can truly "pierce" the innermost being (Hebrews

4:12), and it is only by the Holy Spirit that human beings can utter the Word of God.

6. *Love of the Scriptures.* A regular characteristic of charismatic witnesses is a new love for the Word of God. Bible reading becomes exciting and rewarding, for people baptized in the Spirit find meaning "jumping out" at them from the biblical books. It is rather like the experience of the disciples on the road to Emmaus, "Did not our hearts burn within us while he [Jesus] talked to us on the road, while he opened to us the scriptures?" (Luke 24:32). This is the experience of the Holy Spirit within the believer making contact with the Holy Spirit in the Word of God. There is now something within the Christian (the Holy Spirit at the center of the person's being) that can penetrate the meaning of the Scriptures and open up the life hidden in the sacred text.

So people who may have labored away at bible reading for years and felt it was all very complicated (all these genealogies, lists of kings, complex teachings on law and gospel, justification and righteousness, too much blood) with confusion rather than light as the usual result, now find the key to its meaning. The Spirit opens the mind (Luke 24:45) to reveal Christ as the center of the Scriptures, "he interpreted to them in all the scriptures the things concerning himself" (Luke 24:27). This knowledge brings life.

7. *Fuller Freedom from Sin.* Charismatic testimonies regularly tell of the baptism in the Holy Spirit bringing a new degree of freedom from sin. People often describe how this surge of new life in Jesus suddenly banished the remains of some sinful habit, which the efforts of years had never managed to eradicate. Others tell how the grace of the "baptism" released them from bondage to fears of other people's opinions, and gave them a freedom to act as disciples—to witness, to speak out, to serve. The new love for Jesus that comes with this grace makes a real dent in people's love for the things of this world.

A major instrument in God's hands for spreading this blessing has been David Wilkerson's book *The Cross and the Switchblade.* This dramatic story thrilled millions as they heard how the lives of young addicts in New York City were transformed from violence, degradation and hopelessness to compassion, dignity and holy purpose through the power of God in the baptism in the Spirit. Readers instinctively sensed, "If God can free them from such bondage, then he can surely free me from my sins."

8. *Spiritual Gifts.* Charismatic testimonies bear witness to those gifts or charisms that Paul lists in 1 Corinthians 12:8-10. Particularly noteworthy here are the gifts of prophecy, of healing and of speaking with other tongues. These are often the elements that "outsiders" see as the distinguishing marks of the movement. It is true that they are distinctive of the Pentecostal and charismatic movements, and the witnesses testify to their importance, and the difference they make.

In fact, these gifts fit in perfectly with the characteristics already mentioned. Prophecy manifests in a striking way that God still speaks to his people today. Prophecy in the first person, as a word from the Lord, makes it very clear that when people are saying the Lord speaks to them, they do not just mean that a vague idea came into their mind. The living God truly spoke. And the word can be tested, and countless testimonies tell of the fruit that came from words of prophecy.

Healing manifests in a clear way that the power of God is no less today than in the first century A.D. Jesus Christ truly is "the same yesterday and today and for ever" (Hebrews 13:8). Healing of a physical kind makes visible for those with little or no faith the reality of Jesus Christ, of his love and his mercy for suffering humankind.

The gift of tongues is constantly experienced as a gift of praise. Charismatic testimonies speak of people uttering words they did not understand, but knowing that they were praising God from the depths of their being. Witnesses often show how speaking in tongues was experienced as expressing something to God going beyond what the mind could think and what one's vocabulary could express. This is another important aspect of baptism in the Spirit: that the coming of the Spirit brings back an awareness of the mystery of God, of how far God exceeds our human minds and pretensions. Through the coming of the Holy Spirit, God again becomes truly God for us: the Almighty, all-loving, all-wise God is recognized as the Almighty Lord of all creation, before whom all flesh must bow in penitence and humble adoration.

9. *"Come, Lord Jesus."* When people are baptized in the Spirit, the "last things"—heaven, hell, judgment—are no longer mere theories to be discussed, but realities that face us mortal creatures. They know that here on this earth they have no abiding city and "they desire a better country, that is, a heavenly one" (Hebrews 11:16). In particular they have a living hope in the New Testament promise of the return of Jesus at the end of world history. Because they have tasted "the first fruits of the Spirit" (Romans 8:23) and know something of the reality of Jesus Christ, they long for the time when the present inner tension between spirit and flesh will be finished. Thus they "groan inwardly as [they] wait for adoption as sons" (Romans 8:23), looking for the day when they will no longer see "in a mirror dimly, but then face to face" (1 Corinthians 13:12). People baptized in the Spirit are a people who pray, "Come, Lord Jesus" (Revelation 22:20).

Chapter Four

A New Thing

SO FAR WE HAVE SAMPLED SOME WITNESSES OF HOW THE Lord dramatically changed lives through the baptism in the Spirit; we have seen how it all began, both in America and in Europe; and we have looked at the wonderful effects of this blessing. Now we are in a position to look at the whole movement and ask such questions as: How important is this move of the Spirit? What does it represent in God's sight? Is it the kind of grace the Lord has poured out on most generations in the history of the church, or is it something more unusual and more remarkable?

We can look now at the characteristics of this movement that are most striking and that indicate something of the divine purpose. As we do this, let us have a reverence for God's work, and know we can only understand the work of the Spirit through the enlightenment of the same Spirit. As Paul says, "no one comprehends the thoughts of God except the Spirit of God" (1 Corinthians 2:11).

Holy Spirit of God, you who search all things, even the depths of God, you through whom the Incarnate Son of God took human flesh and grew in wisdom and knowledge, fill our minds now, and enable us to transcend the limitations of earthly thinking to penetrate the mystery of the divine will and purpose. Help us to see your hand in this movement that bears your imprint; show us what is eternal, what is of you, so that we may respond in the only fitting way to this marvelous grace.

1. *Unplanned and Unexpected.* When men and women began to be blessed by God in this way, it was in almost all cases a total surprise. A few had been led to know that there was much more

to receive from God, and this knowledge spurred their search. But virtually none had any idea that this could be God's way of renewing his people. Even though "renewal" was much discussed in many church circles, especially among Catholics in connection with the Second Vatican Council (1962-65), no renewal groups had the idea that what their church needed was baptism in the Spirit and spiritual gifts!

It is true that the Catholic bishops at Vatican II amended a draft document on the church to make clear that the charismata (by which they meant much more than the gifts of 1 Corinthians 12:8-10) are bestowed throughout the church and are not merely extraordinary gifts. Certainly this can be seen as part of the Holy Spirit's preparation of the Roman Catholic Church to accept and welcome the charismatic movement. But it does not mean that any Catholic bishops were actually anticipating the restoration of the spiritual gifts found in the renewal.

The charismatic renewal in its origins was not planned, but simply happened. It was an unexpected event or series of events, not the actualizing of a theory. What struck people was what was happening in people's lives. They heard or read of burdened lives finding relief and hope; they heard or read of healings, of remarkable interventions of the Lord that showed his personal love and his power. They were faced by acts of God, that posed the question: Do you recognize God's hand here? Do you believe he can do the same for you? They were not faced at first by an organized movement in the church. At the beginning there were no programs, no Life in the Spirit seminars, no service committees for charismatic renewal. The question facing people was not, "What do I think of this new church movement?" but "How do I respond to the evident signs of God's intervention in people's lives?"

The only people who believed that the spiritual gifts are part of the basic equipment of the church for its full mission were the Pentecostals. But they tended to regard the gifts as "theirs" and with very few exceptions had no expectation that these would ever break out and find a place within the historic denominations. David du Plessis was one of these few, and through Wigglesworth's prophecy he believed that God would pour out his Spirit on all flesh, including all the churches. But du Plessis knew he could not initiate it, and he had to wait on the Lord. His role was to be a witness when the Lord began. He could then say, "That which you are now receiving is the baptism in the Spirit. This is what the Pentecostals received at the start of the century and which was meant for the whole church."

2. *No Human Founder and No One Place of Origin.* It is possible, as we have seen in Chapter Two, to trace back this renewal to some of its earliest manifestations. But the more you try to track down its origins, the more you find it cannot be traced back to any one person or place of origin. This work of God was a totally unexpected event, neither an idea whose hour has come nor a theory that was being put into practice. There are no human pioneer founder figures in the renewal. No one first had the idea that this kind of movement was what the church really needed, and then tried to put it into effect. Interestingly, the only example in church history of someone having the idea that the full range of spiritual gifts was what the church needed, and who then sought to bring this about, was the Scotsman Edward Irving in London in the 1820s, and it did not work out.

Thus the pioneer figures were not in any way the authors of the movement. They were all people to whom something happened, something beyond their expectations, something wonderful and glorious, in which they were surprisingly caught up. Some of them were thrust into positions of leadership, for which they had not sought and for which they felt themselves ill-prepared. The best-known names among the pioneers, people like Dennis Bennett, Larry Christenson, Michael Harper, were not at the very beginning any more prominent than men like Richard Winkler, Frank Maguire and Philip Smith, whose names are probably unknown to most charismatics. The reason why men like Bennett, Christenson and Harper became internationally-recognized leaders was what they did with their gift and call, staking their futures on this work of God. At the beginning, there were simply Christians scattered here and there, some in positions of responsibility, others in humbler circumstances, but all touched by the Lord in the same distinctive way, and for all of whom this intervention of God was mysterious and beyond their capacity fully to understand.

3. *No Single Way into This Blessing.* There was no standard way of people coming to receive the baptism in the Spirit. In fact, there were a remarkable number of different ways in which the Lord led people into this blessing.

Some heard about "the baptism" from the Pentecostals, like Harald Bredesen, and the many people who read David Wilkerson's *The Cross and the Switchblade.* Some were led into this reality by prayerful study of the New Testament, especially the Acts of the Apostles, like the Methodist Tommy Tyson in North Carolina and some of the first Catholics at Duquesne. Some experienced the gifts of the Spirit after intensive prayer for revival, as with groups in Britain like the Nights of Prayer for World-Wide Revival. Many rediscovered the power of God in healing. Some of these were evangelicals, first discovering the prominence of healing in the New Testament, and then becoming aware of other spiritual gifts besides healing. Others were more liturgical and sacramental, first discovering the power of God in the anointing of the sick, and so being opened up to believe in the immediacy of God's presence and power (this was true of Bill Wood in the London Healing Mission). For others the introduction was more dramatic, through actually being healed (like Edgar Trout of England, immobile after a serious accident, and Sister Briege McKenna from Ireland, healed of rheumatoid arthritis), or by being used unexpectedly in the healing of another. Besides all these, there were simply cases of people who had never heard of the baptism in the Spirit, who had never sought any such experience, suddenly being touched by the Lord and finding themselves baptized in the Spirit, and praising God in other tongues. One dramatic instance at a small Mennonite church in Minnesota in the mid-1950s is told by Gerald Derstine in his book *Following the Fire*.

The multiplicity of ways by which God led people into the baptism in the Spirit reinforces the fact that the movement has no human founder. While people's starting points were so different, and their ways of entry so varied, the reality into which they were being led was the same. In all this variety, we can sense a common purpose, the saving, sanctifying, liberating work of God.

4. *Across All the Churches*. Even before this move of the Spirit became public with the testimony of Dennis Bennett in 1960, men and women from a wide variety of church backgrounds were being touched. Bredesen, from a Lutheran background, had accepted a Dutch Reformed pastorate. Tyson was a Methodist, Derstine a Mennonite. Jim Brown pastored a Presbyterian church, while Agnes Sanford quietly led the way among Episcopalians. John Osteen was a Baptist. Soon the movement was found in virtually every Protestant body in North America.

It was fitting that David du Plessis was the instrument used by God to gather together for the first time those Americans from so many traditions who had been baptized in the Spirit. This happened near Columbus, Ohio, in the fall of 1962, when forty ministers came together: Congregational, Reformed, Mennonite, Lutheran, Episcopal, Baptist, Methodist, Presbyterian and Pentecostal.

In Europe, too, a comparable range can be seen, even from the early stages. In Holland, the *Vuur* movement begun in 1957 soon included pastors from both major Reformed churches, from the Baptists, the Remonstrant brotherhood and as early as 1963 a Roman Catholic priest. In Britain, pastors and clergy from a range of traditions were brought together when David du Plessis visited in the summer of 1964. Among those who gathered to hear "Mr. Pentecost" were Anglicans of all patterns of churchmanship, Baptists, a Methodist, a minister from the Church of Scotland, and a group of independents, mostly ex-Plymouth Brethren. The participation of John Gunstone, from the Anglo—Catholic wing of the Church of England, showed clearly that this movement was reaching beyond the circles of evangelical Protestantism.

But it was with the dramatic outbreak of this movement in the Roman Catholic Church in early 1967 that its unprecedented range became unmistakable. Never before since the division that rent Western Christendom in the sixteenth century had Protestants and Catholics been brought into the same movement of revival and renewal. This was not like getting Catholics and Protestants to have a common service for peace or some other cause of mutual concern. Both were being equally touched by the same unexpected grace. People from both sides were being so grasped by the Spirit of God that they were all able to worship God together in a way that neither could before.

Another point to note is the speed with which this movement has traveled across the world. In every country to which it has come, some have been brought into this blessing in a sovereign manner, without hearing of it from others, and only later discovering that others have had the same experience.

The "new thing" that is a spiritual revival found equally in every tradition is symbolized by the rise of many ecumenical communities through the renewal. These communities, like Word of God, Ann Arbor, Michigan; Alleluia Community, Augusta, Georgia; People of Praise, South Bend, Indiana; Mother of God Community, near Washington, D.C. and Chemin Neuf, Lyon, France, are possible because the Holy Spirit has done an identical thing in the lives of all members, of whatever church tradition. This shared grace has here resulted in a common life in a way that was not possible before.

5. *Not Belonging to Any One Church.* This short study of the origins of this move of the Holy Spirit shows clearly that it does not belong to any one church or denomination. It is a sovereign work of God across all the churches and all the traditions. That is what is so remarkable and so exciting. This was one of the wonders at the big Kansas City conference in 1977 and it will surely be one of the memorable dimensions of the New Orleans conference in July, 1987.

The fact of not being tied to any one tradition is closely linked with the movement having no one human founder. For all the great church movements that were hatched by the Spirit in the mind of a human leader have been marked by the church background of that leader. Only a movement sent straight from heaven without obvious human founders could belong equally to every Christian church and tradition. Only then could we know that being baptized in the Spirit is not turning Catholics into Protestants or Protestants into Pentecostals.

An important consequence of the charismatic movement not belonging to any one church tradition is its unity. Or perhaps we should put it the other way round and say: an important consequence of the spiritual unity of the movement is that it doesn't belong to any one church tradition more than another. This means that there is not a separate movement of Catholic charismatic renewal, another of Episcopalian renewal, another of Lutheran, etc. No, in the sense of movement of the Holy Spirit, there is only one movement, and it is found among Baptists, Catholics, Episcopalians, Lutherans, Mennonites, Methodists, Presbyterians, etc. When we talk about Anglican, Baptist, Catholic, Lutheran charismatic renewal, we must be careful to remember that we are not talking about a separate movement in our own church, but only that segment of one ecumenical move of the Spirit that is found in our own tradition.

God calls us to bear witness to his work, and this means bearing witness to people in our own church traditions of this ecumenical work of the Spirit. We have to be true to "the facts of the Holy Spirit." When Catholic charismatics speak only of the movement beginning in 1967, without mentioning Protestant antecedents, they are not really being faithful to what God has done and how he has done it. The same holds true for Protestant charismatics whose histories make no mention of God's work among the Pentecostals. The most faithful accounts are those that bear witness to the full story of how the Lord poured out his Spirit among the Pentecostals, especially at Azusa Street, and how after they were expelled from their churches or not made welcome, they formed independent assemblies and new denominations. But now in the charismatic outpouring from the 1950s the Lord has begun to bring this great grace back into the historic traditions, first the Protestant and then the Catholic. This is faithfully described in books like Michael Harper's *As at the Beginning* and Vinson Synan's *Charismatic Bridges*.

We may say then that this pentecostal movement of the Spirit is inherently ecumenical, that it is an ecumenical grace of new life for the churches. To say it is ecumenical means two things in particular:

(I) it is for all the churches equally; all need it; God gives it freely to all;

(II) it is a grace that will unify. As Christians from all churches respond to this grace, they will be brought into unity by the Holy Spirit of God.

The implications of this ecumenical grace will be further explored in the following chapters.

CHAPTER FIVE

A Grace to Build On

As a sovereign movement of the Holy Spirit without any human founder, the charismatic renewal differs significantly from all those movements among Christians that trace themselves back to the ideas and inspiration of dedicated and often visionary pioneer figures. Looking into these differences more closely will throw light on the distinctiveness of this work of the Holy Spirit.

All church traditions are familiar with organized movements of revival and renewal. In God's mercy and love, he never leaves his people in their weakness and sin, but continually seeks to recall them to the gospel of life. In the centuries of separation, these movements of the Spirit of God have taken somewhat different forms. The Catholic movements have tended to produce new organizations, many of them new religious orders, within the Roman Catholic Church, while the Protestant movements tended, though not in all cases, to produce para-church organizations or new denominations. A comparison between the charismatic movement and these other works of the Lord will help to make clearer the exceptional grace represented by this ecumenical work of the Holy Spirit.

The Catholic Church in the twentieth century has been particularly blessed by a number of renewal movements that have provided the spiritual impetus and the means for many to find new life in Christ. Obvious examples are the Focolari (founded in Northern Italy during World War II by Chiara Lubich to promote the unity and peace of people through union with Jesus Christ); the Legion of Mary (founded in the 1930s in Ireland by Frank Duff to form lay apostles from among the ordinary members of the

Catholic Church); the Cursillo movement (founded in Spain by Bishop Hervas at the end of the 1940s to provide a method for Catholics to live the basic gospel message in the church); the Movement for a Better World (founded by Fr. Riccardo Lombardi in the mid-1950s in Rome to mobilize young people to transform the world and its future through conversion to Christ); Comunione e Liberazione (founded in Italy by Fr. Luigi Giussani in 1954 to form microcosms of the church in which people find liberation through communion in Christ).

Among Protestants, some movements like the Salvation Army have led in effect to new denominations. But others have grown within a particular denomination (like the Church Army among Anglicans and the Haugean revival movement within the Lutheran Church of Norway) or have spanned the Protestant churches (like the renowned Taizé community in France and in a different way organizations like Operation Mobilization, Youth with a Mission, and Campus Crusade).

For all their great variety, all these organized movements follow a similar pattern. They were started by a person of faith and energy, who saw a particular need among the Christian people, in their own church or simply in surrounding society. The founder gathered a group of like-minded Christians with whom the vision was shared. Often despite trials and oppositions, a new organized movement was born, embodying the vision of the founder and offering some plan, method or way of life reflecting the wisdom and experience of the founder. Vision, ideal and method typify all these movements. These organized movements are thus decisively influenced by the personal charism and the thinking of their founders. Such movements typically belong to and reflect strongly the church tradition of the founder.

In all these movements with human founders, there are forms of explicit membership and enrollment. Ordinarily, members commit themselves to some basic spiritual discipline, such as daily pattern of prayer, regular study of the scriptures or regular participation in the eucharist, acceptance of some basic statutes. Becoming a member involves receiving some spiritual formation from more experienced members. Though many of these movements are not trying to bring all others into their own organization but are simply seeking to bring them new life through the gospel, the instruments of this new life are the dedicated and spiritually formed members committed to their movement and its methods.

Here we can see a major difference from the charismatic renewal. People do not join the charismatic movement. They become part of this work of the Spirit by baptism in the Spirit, which may occur anywhere—in your kitchen, in a prayer group or in your bath (David du Plessis is said to have recommended seeking in your bath, as it is a time of greater relaxation!). Even though the renewal in the Holy Spirit has become more organized with time, the movement is still wider than the sum total of charismatic groups and communities.

Another difference is that members of the organized movements are often more spiritually mature than the average charismatic. For the programs of formation in the organized movements assist maturity and help to weed out unstable people with obvious emotional problems. Much wisdom from the spiritual traditions of the past has gone into the shaping of the organized movements, especially those with strong denominational backing. Aside from the covenant communities, there is very little in the charismatic renewal by way of required spiritual formation as a condition for "belonging." The spiritual maturity of charismatics is largely dependent on the maturity of the charismatic groups they attend. These vary far more widely than local groups within the organized movements, which have prescribed patterns and forms of training.

However, the charismatic movement has manifested a presence of God's power greater than has characterized the organized movements. Everywhere the charismatic renewal has come, there has been a manifestation of the power of the Spirit—

in healings, in dramatic conversions, in words of knowledge, in various forms of divine intervention. It is this manifestation of power that attracts the most needy, just as all the most troubled in Palestine flocked to hear Jesus, sensing hope of salvation. It is as though the grace of baptism in the Spirit is more powerful and less restricted. Not being first mediated through human understanding, it involves a directness of encounter with the living God. It is as though a more potent gift has been entrusted to the less trained. These factors point to the charismatic renewal having a potential greater than the other renewal movements but also with a far higher risk that its potential will not be realized. For realization of its potential depends on charismatics becoming mature, and being faithful to the more powerful grace they have received.

Being faithful to the grace of the "baptism" has another dimension that should be noted, as it will be taken up in later chapters. The organized movements bring with them their own self-understanding. If you want to know what is the meaning of Focolari, you read the writings of Chiara Lubich. If you want to understand the Legion of Mary, you read its handbook. If you want to understand the aims and ideals of Taizé, you examine the rule and read the writings of Brother Roger Schutz. In other words, you find out the basic meaning and thrust of a movement by studying the mind and vision of the founder. But with the charismatic renewal, there is no human founder whose mind and ideas we can study. Since its author is the Lord, we have to seek out the mind of the Lord, if we are to grasp the meaning and purpose of the movement. Therefore one of the major elements in determining whether charismatics are faithful or unfaithful to the grace of baptism in the Spirit is their earnestness in seeking the mind of the Lord. It is only possible to be faithful to the grace of the renewal if we seek out from the Lord what it means and why he has sent it.

Another difference between the organized movements and the renewal in the Holy Spirit is that the former usually have some particular focus. They may be directed to student milieux, like Campus Crusade and Youth with a Mission. They may be directed toward married couples, like Marriage Encounter. They may presume a certain level of education. They may be concerned with the formation of leaders. Besides these differences of *who* the movements aim to recruit, there are often limitations or specifications as to *what* they are aiming to achieve. Some may focus on personal spiritual formation, some on family life, others on public worship, yet others on social involvement. By contrast, in the charismatic renewal God has been touching every kind of person: grandmothers as well as teenagers, the illiterate as well as the literate, priests, contemplative religious, and even those outside all the churches. Its scope cannot be restricted to one aspect of church life, such as family, worship, evangelism, lay apostolate, catechesis, or personal spiritual formation. The range of spiritual fruit coming from the renewal touches every aspect of church life. This work of the Spirit is as wide as the heart of God, even wider than any one church. So while the charismatic renewal characteristically transforms public worship and issues in spontaneous praise, it also transforms catechesis, making alive the presence of the indwelling Spirit in both teacher and taught. Likewise, through the renewal, the Lord has been working profound changes in family life, uniting husbands and wives on the basis of their common knowledge of Jesus and the power of his cross. Thus, charismatic renewal has no characteristic techniques and methods. Its constant message concerns the work of the Trinity, accepting the Son and his saving work through the Spirit to bring us to the Father.

It is then a serious misunderstanding to bracket the charismatic renewal with other renewal movements of an organized kind, as though it were simply another form of the same kind of thing. To say this is not to denigrate the organized movements. They have probably made a greater contribution to the renewal of Christian life in our countries than any other recent factors prior to the charismatic renewal. Moreover, these organizations have often been valuable training-grounds for people who later became key leaders in the charismatic renewal. Men like Ralph Martin and Steve Clark of the Word of God Community learned much of their basic discipline and methodology from their years in the Cursillo movement. Cursillo not only prepared them for the grace of baptism in the Spirit, but it also helped them to know what to do after they had received it. Experience in the organized movements would typically inculcate a strong sense of the need for formation and provide pointers on how to lead people to maturity.

The main points from these comparisons show that the charismatic movement is a grace of God touching every aspect of the Christian life and is found across all the Christian churches. It does not, however, bring with it an automatic understanding of its meaning. It does not bring with it any inbuilt program for maturing recipients. The initial outpouring of the charismatic renewal is an act of creation that has later to be shaped and built upon. The renewal is not just an unprecedented gift. It is also an unprecedented task.

CHAPTER SIX

What Does It Mean?

As we look at these facts about the renewal in the Holy Spirit, its history, its salient characteristics, and its unusual features, we need to ask, "What does it mean?" The first question of course is, "Is this from God?" We can look at fruits such as awareness of the Trinity, knowledge of Jesus, praise of God, evangelism, and know that these are basic works of the Spirit of God. So at this point we have a basis for recognizing, "Yes, this movement, whatever its imperfections, is a work of God." So the next question is that of meaning and purpose. What does it mean in God's plan and purpose?

As we consider this question, we must again remember that it is only by the Spirit of God that we can understand the things of God. God's purpose in pouring out this sovereign grace is not going to be grasped and understood simply by brilliant minds, by theological Einsteins, whose intellectual genius opens up the unknown. This spiritual understanding will only come as the fruit of prayer. The Lord will only open up his mind to believers with humble minds, who acknowledge their own incapacity and need before him. The words of Jesus about his message are applicable here, "I thank you, Father, Lord of heaven and earth, that you have hidden these things from the wise and understanding and revealed them to babes" (Matthew 11:25). What God reveals to the humble has its own divine simplicity that the person who does not know the Lord cannot grasp.

Let us then prayerfully look at the evidence to see what this outpouring of the Spirit means in God's sight. Many people studying this movement notice first what clearly distinguishes it from other movements, namely the rediscovery or reappearance of the spiritual gifts listed in 1 Corinthians 12: words of wisdom and knowledge, faith, gifts of healing, the working of miracles, prophecy, the ability to distinguish between spirits, various kinds of tongues, and interpretation of tongues. However, from those within the movement, there is a constant witness that while the gifts are important, they do not form its heart or core-element.

This is an important point of evidence in the search for the movement's meaning. The witnesses all point to baptism in the Spirit as its heart or core. Nonetheless, everyone recognizes that if there had been no outpouring of the spiritual gifts, there would have been no charismatic movement as we know it. There is then some kind of essential link between the baptism in the Spirit and the spiritual gifts.

As we wonder how important this movement is, we should notice an important point about these gifts of the Spirit. They provide an example of something very unusual in Christian history: the restoration of something clearly present in the New Testament but largely absent during the greater part of Christian history. Many scholars have tried to show that these gifts were not totally lost between the third and the twentieth centuries, but their studies only reinforce the importance of their reappearance. For the occasional occurrence of these gifts in the past shows that they were not seen as part of the normal God-given equipment of each local church. The reappearance of the spiritual gifts thus represents something dramatically new in church history. Once you admit they are authentic and are the work of the Holy Spirit, you have to recognize that something of possibly unparalleled importance is happening.

In other words, if God is truly restoring to the church something that has not been present as he purposed since say the third century A.D., then what we are witnessing is more than just another renewal movement that injects a bit of extra spiritual dynamism into the church. It is something much more radical.

This conclusion is supported by the unexpected rise of charismatic Jewish Christians in what many call "Messianic Judaism." These are Jews converted to faith in Jesus Christ as the Messiah, but who retain their Jewish identity and form Christian synagogues. Estimates put their numbers in the U.S.A. as between 30,000 and 50,000, an astonishing figure in such a short span of time. Here too something unknown since the second century is reappearing, a form of Jewish Christianity.

These pointers to the extraordinary significance of this work of the Spirit are not logical conclusions with a mathematical certainty to force down the throats of other Christians. They are indicators to take to prayer. We need to say to the Lord: "Lord, these are the signs we see. Correct us if we are mistaken. Open up to us the divine purpose in what you are showing us."

The Heart of This Movement

What is it that is common to baptism in the Spirit and the spiritual gifts? What is basic to them that is not just the outer shell, but is the inner core and heart? We can here distinguish between what belongs to the order of *means* (how God works in the renewal) and what belongs to the order of *content* (what we receive through these means).

The Means. One immediate striking feature of the renewal in the Holy Spirit, one that can often irritate other Christians, is the way participants talk about God. They speak quite casually of God telling them this or that, and of God intervening in their lives. "I just didn't know what to say to him. So I prayed, and suddenly an image of a sad child came to me. I asked him about his childhood, and he opened up to me about his whole life." "I was completely lost, so I turned to the Lord, and the very next moment, I saw the place I was looking for." Participants in this renewal typically experience a new directness of relationship to God.

This directness operates in both directions. There is a new directness in God's relationship to us, and in our relationship to him. We can look in turn at these two aspects, which are manifested in a new ability to hear God and a new ability to worship God.

First, we can examine that feature of charismatic witnesses noted in Chapter Three that "God speaks to us." We can call this inner revelation, or revelation in the Spirit (1 Corinthians 2:9-10). At baptism in the Spirit something happens that opens up a new level of communication between the believer and the Trinity. God is no longer a distant figure behind the scenes. He is truly revealed in one's deepest being as "Father," one who addresses by name those he calls as his sons and daughters. Jesus is known as our mighty Savior, who truly delivers from all evil, and as living Lord, who always continues to exercise his all-powerful authority. There is consciously new life within the Christian. At the heart of this transformation is the experience of hearing the Lord, of knowing that God speaks to his children personally and desires to open his mind to them.

This divine speaking can take a variety of forms. It is not always the equivalent of hearing a "voice." Sometimes, it comes through passages of Scripture that leap out at the reader, maybe speaking exactly to their current situation and answering precisely the question they had put before the Lord. Sometimes an impression that is clear and stable appears within the believer, maybe a word or phrase, maybe an image or picture. Jesus says of the disciples who form his flock that they know the voice of the shepherd (John 10:4). "I am the good shepherd; I know my own and my own know me" (John 10:14). It is part of spiritual growth that we learn how to hear and recognize the voice of the divine shepherd.

Some of the spiritual gifts are particular forms of the Lord speaking to his people, for example, prophecy, the word of wisdom, and the word of knowledge. These gifts are only different in that here the message from the Lord is not simply for the hearer, but is to be transmitted to others for the upbuilding of the body of Christ.

There is plenty of evidence from Christian history of holy people hearing the Lord. But inner revelation was not something expected by ordinary believers. And not even the holy people were expecting the spiritual gifts. If they came, as they occasionally did, they were seen as a divine bonus, to be gratefully received perhaps, but not to be sought. With the restoration of inner revelation in the Spirit through the baptism in the Spirit, this directness of relationship to God is being restored to ordinary Christians as part of normal Christian life. The reappearance of the gifts is a visible sign of this restoration. It is making clear that God is a Father who speaks to all his children. The gifts emphasize that the Lord speaks to individuals for the sake of the whole church. Hearing the Lord is not a private privilege, but a grace and a responsibility of each Christian as a member of the body of Christ.

This restoration of inner revelation to the church is recalling us to the full meaning of the term *apokalupsis* in the New Testament. For this Greek work, almost always translated *revelation* (it literally means unveiling), refers in the New Testament both to what is revealed (Romans 1:18; 16:25) and to how it is revealed. Passages in Galatians and Ephesians clearly refer to the manner in which God spoke, "For I did not receive it from man, nor was I taught it, but it came through a revelation of Jesus Christ" (Galatians 1:12) and "the mystery was made known to me by revelation" (Ephesians 3:3).

Over the centuries the Christian use of the term "revelation" has come to refer almost wholly to the content, and hardly at all to the directness of God's means of communication. For both Catholics and evangelical Protestants, revelation has come to refer to the objective body of teaching given by God in salvation history. Many people then assumed that revelation reaches the church today in a less direct way than was experienced by the first Christians: either in the view of evangelical Protestants straight out of the Bible or in the view of Catholics and Orthodox through transmission by each successive generation. God sent Jesus, Jesus taught the twelve, the twelve taught their successors, and way down the line their successors teach us. The renewal in the Holy Spirit is now showing us that both these positions overlooked the role of the Holy Spirit.

The Holy Spirit is God's instrument in revelation. In the coming of Jesus, both the content and the means were new. Since the completion of the content of revelation in the incarnation and glorification of the Son of God, the revealing work of the Holy Spirit is to take that objective Word, the teaching of the Scriptures, the reality of Jesus Christ, and bring this to life in the mind and heart of each believer. This does not mean that there is no role for a teaching church. But it is clear that each new generation receiving the message of the gospel is to have the same direct access to God as the first. Each generation in the church is meant to know the revealing work of the Holy Spirit. Now the content is not new, but the means of giving it to us is the same.

Secondly, we can look briefly at the new directness of our relationship to God. As a result of baptism in the Spirit, we have a new directness in expressing our worship to God. This too is the work of the Holy Spirit within the believer. Worship is not just joining in an objective rite, nor is it simply making up our own prayers. It is being moved by the indwelling Holy Spirit in ways that exceed our natural powers of mind and intellect. This is expressed by the apostle Paul, "Likewise the Spirit helps us in our weakness; for we do not know how to pray as we ought, but the Spirit himself intercedes for us with sighs too deep for words" (Romans 8:26).

This directness of expression in worship to God is also made visible in a striking way through the spiritual gift of speaking in other tongues. For the gift of tongues enables the Christian to express the worship of the inner spirit without even the mediation of the mind. Not even my ideas then come between me and the Lord. This gift, like the word gifts already mentioned, crystallizes something that is in fact true of all Christian life. It makes clear that all Christian worship is an activity of the Holy Spirit. It shows the Spirit raising the believer above natural capacities to direct heart-felt worship and adoration of the infinite God revealed in his only Son. This renewal is then restoring to the church the full role of the Holy Spirit in worship, a role that is dependent on the full yielding of the Christian's being to Jesus in the baptism in the Spirit.

The Content. If revelation through the Spirit is the means by which God communicates with the believer who has been baptized in the Spirit, what is it that the Spirit reveals? The experience of those baptized in the Spirit corresponds to what is described by Jesus in John's gospel, "But when the Counselor comes, whom I shall send to you from the Father, even the Spirit of truth, who proceeds from the Father, he will bear witness to me." (John 15:26).

The witnesses constantly point to a new level of knowledge of Jesus. They often contain revelation of the meaning of the cross, manifesting the infinite love of the Savior, who died for us sinners. Jesus is made known as the victor on the cross, and as the risen Lord, who now exercises all authority in heaven and on earth. As a Presbyterian pastor testified to his church authorities: "I wish I could adequately share with you and help you to understand what happened to me. It was not "something"—not just an experience—but it was Someone who happened to me. There came into my life an inward reality, an inner presence, that is nothing less than Jesus Christ himself."

As we look at such testimonies, we can see how Jesus is at the center. Jesus' words, "I am the way, the truth and the life" (John 14:6), are borne out in the experience of baptism in the Spirit. Those baptized in the Spirit have found Jesus as the way to the

Father, they have discovered that he is the truth, and this truth that is Jesus has brought them life, eternal life. As we pray about the testimonies, we can sense how the new relationship with Jesus is the cause of all the other blessings. The ability and desire to praise God, the new power to evangelize, the love of the Scriptures, the greater freedom from sin, the reception of spiritual gifts, all are the result of the new relationship with Jesus, not the other way round.

The evidence shows that at baptism in the Spirit the Spirit opens up a new relationship with Jesus Christ, so that recipients know Jesus as Savior and as Lord in the innermost part of their being. This relationship means new life, the life in the Spirit. That is why the renewal is not just a movement touching one segment of church life, like liturgy or mission, but encompasses everything. With this new knowledge of Jesus, everything that is of God comes to new life: the Scriptures, the liturgy and sacraments, personal prayer, ministry and preaching, relationships, family life, youth work. Likewise it confirms that this work of God is for people of all ages, races, cultures and backgrounds. Knowledge of Jesus Christ in the inner spirit through the Holy Spirit is not reserved for the educated, or for the upper and middle class; it is for all. So this renewal is found in all continents among people of every kind, reaching the poor and uneducated in a way that movements based on human ideas never can.

It is significant that Christians touched by the Holy Spirit in this movement constantly prefer the term "baptism in the Holy Spirit" to describe the basic grace which they have received. Despite the objections of scholars and theologians worried about confusion with baptism in water, they have always sensed that other suggested terms like "infilling" and "effusion" do not fit in the same way as "baptism." The main reason for this preference is probably twofold: first, the scriptural association between baptism in the Spirit and the event of Pentecost (Acts 1:5, 11:16-17) and second, the association between baptism and

WHAT DOES IT MEAN?

death (Romans 6:3-5). For being opened to this new level of direct relationship with the persons of the Trinity is impossible without a surrender, without a dying to self-sufficiency and self-regulation.

This examination of the meaning of the movement has led us to see inner revelation as the means, and the person and mission of Jesus as the content. Where does power come in? Many have seen power as the characteristic mark of the charismatic renewal, believing this to be the promise actualized at Pentecost: "behold, I send the promise of my Father upon you: but stay in the city, until you are clothed with power from on high" (Luke 24:49). It is totally true that the power of God characterizes this renewal. Often the works of power are what initially attract attention and make the most impression. However, this short analysis suggests that what is most fundamental about the renewal is not power, but the basis for that power, namely the new level of relationship with the Lord that brings new life.

What was promised was not simply power, but the promise of the Father. And the promise is the Holy Spirit. The Holy Spirit is the very life of God. It is impossible to receive this abundant life without deeper surrender to Jesus Christ the Lord.

Experience in the renewal confirms the danger of any focus on power that is not subordinated to Christians' relationship to the persons of the Trinity. To some who say to Jesus, "Lord, did we not prophesy in your name, and cast out demons in your name, and do many mighty works in your name?" the Lord replies, "I never knew you; depart from me, you evildoers" (Matthew 7:22-23).

The meaning and significance of the Lord baptizing believers in his Holy Spirit is that it is restoring to the whole church that means and level of knowledge of himself that characterized the Christians of the apostolic age. The spiritual gifts that follow on the baptism in the Spirit make clear in a striking and visible way the directness of God's working among his people, and that these divine endowments are intended as the normal equipment for each local church. With the new knowledge of the Lord comes clarity about the dignity and responsibility of being his sons and daughters. With this living relationship comes the full power and equipment of the Holy Spirit to fulfill the mission of the church.

Part II

HOLY SPIRIT RENEWAL AND THE CHRISTIAN CHURCHES

Chapter Seven

Present Outpouring and Past Traditions

So far, we have focused on this charismatic renewal in the Holy Spirit, what it is and what marks it out from other currents and developments in the churches. Now we can ask, What is its relationship to the churches? What ought its relationship to the churches be?

Because the charismatic renewal has sprung up all over the world in virtually every Christian tradition, this question involves all the Christian churches and denominations. A similar question faces all their members who have been baptized in the Spirit. The questions are not: how does the Anglican charismatic renewal relate to the Anglican Communion; how does the Catholic charismatic renewal relate to the Roman Catholic Church; how does the Lutheran charismatic renewal relate to the Lutheran Churches, etc. For in the origin of this work of God, there were not separate denominational movements of Holy Spirit renewal. There was one movement of the Holy Spirit touching Christians of every tradition. The real questions are:

For the existing churches:

How do we as churches respond to this one ecumenical movement of God's Holy Spirit?

For participants:

How do we as Christians baptized in the Spirit and part of an ecumenical work of God across all the churches relate this grace to our own church tradition and to our lives as committed church members?

What Faces the Churches?

What faces the churches is the work of the Holy Spirit today, described in the first part of this book. It is the work of the Lord baptizing Christians of all traditions and backgrounds in his Holy Spirit. This is wider than organized forms of what we have come to call charismatic renewal.

Church authorities need to relate to the leaders of charismatic organizations and committees. However, such contacts cannot replace regular contact with people in their own congregations who have been touched by the Holy Spirit in this way. The renewal in the Holy Spirit is people touched and united by God, not primarily organizations and structures.

What Faces the Renewal? Two Opposed Ways of Relating to the Churches

For some Christians, the experience of God in the renewal is so vivid that they have little patience with the apparatus of the churches: their laws, their liturgies, their doctrines, their procedures. For them, their new spiritual union with Christians from very different backgrounds is so evident and exciting that going back into denominational isolation is unthinkable. We are one in the Spirit and we stay one in the Spirit. If the churches get in the way of this, so much the worse for the churches.

Young people may be bored by church affairs, and have no patience with official reasons for continued separation. They may see church barriers in the way of immediate full communion as man-made obstacles the Spirit wants to blast away. People who have been to church for years without evident spiritual fruit may after baptism in the Spirit be indignant that they were never taught these things before. Still others have tried to live out their new life in the Spirit in their local church, but have met so many rebuffs and so little understanding that relating the renewal to their church has seemed a lost cause from the start. These experiences encourage the way of "non-denominationalism," of giving up on the historic churches and making a fresh start. Sometimes the language of "restoration" is used, but for "non-denominationals" restoration means beginning again from scratch, abandoning all hope of repairing and reforming the churches.

For a different group of Christians, church traditions loom large and are very dear to them. They are very conscious of how all that Christianity means to them has come through their own church. Not only is their church their spiritual home, it is the mother that has nourished them with the Word of Life. They will say of their church what the faithful Jews sang of Jerusalem, "This one was born in Zion. . . . All my springs are in you" (Psalm 87:6-7). For these people, leaving or even ignoring their church is unthinkable. Their deepest instinct is to want to live this new life in that church. They want to combine the new "charismatic" elements with all the things in their own tradition that have meant so much over the years. They want to share this new blessing with fellow church members. They have a deep desire for their church to recognize and bless this new movement of the Spirit. Many of these people may live in countries or regions where their church is the dominant faith, and so the ecumenical dimension of the renewal may not be evident to them. For these church people, it is very easy to see their church and its tradition as the fixed order, within which all else has to be accommodated. The importance and centrality of the church tends to mean the importance and centrality of my church. Relating the renewal to the church then means adjusting the renewal to fit that tradition. This is the way of "denominationalism," making an absolute of present church patterns and divisions.

It is important to see that whatever their defects, both these reactions express important truths. As we have seen in Part I, the charismatic renewal is truly a new thing. Here the "non-denominational" sense is right. It is an unprecendented grace of God for all our churches throughout the world. This is a moment of decisive importance for the Christian faith. It is exciting. Through the baptism in the Holy Spirit God has given a real spiritual unity between separated believers. Whom God has united, man should not divide. But it is also true that God has chosen to pour out his saving grace by calling and forming a people to be his own. Though the Christian people and their leaders, like the people of the Old Covenant, are often disobedient and unfaithful, the Lord continues to speak to them and through them. Like all new-born children, Christians enter into an inheritance. Here the "denominational" sense is correct. God has richly blessed every tradition that is founded on his Son, our Lord. He does constantly raise up prophets and holy people to recall his people to his ways. It is a God-given instinct to honor our fathers and mothers in the faith.

However, both reactions contain limitations, and do not easily accept the truth expressed by the other. Both tend to see their own position as authentic and objective, while dismissing the other as primarily emotional and subjective. For those who are so struck by the new unity realized through baptism in the Spirit, people's attachment to church and tradition seems to be sentimental, putting old cherished habits above the call of the Lord. For people deeply loyal to their church and its tradition, the readiness of the other to jettison the churches seems an impulsive and foolhardy response, setting immediate emotions above objective issues of doctrine and the wisdom of centuries.

The Witness of the Scriptures

What do the Scriptures teach us about the tension between God's "new thing" and the wisdom of the ages? In the Scriptures, we see God doing radically new things, but always in a way that builds upon his previous work. As Paul says of the Jewish people, "The gifts and the call are irrevocable" (Romans 11:29).

The Old Testament. The Old Testament is the history of a people to whom a series of promises were made: the promises to

Abraham (Genesis 13:14-17; 15:5; 17:2-8, 16; 22:16-18), to Isaac (Genesis 26:3-5, 24), to Jacob (Genesis 28:13-15; 35:11-12), to Moses (Exodus 19:5-6), to Joshua (Joshua 1:2-9), to David (2 Samuel 7:8-16).

However much the Israelites wandered away from the living God—and they strayed very frequently—God is still the God of Abraham, Isaac and Jacob. The promises made to the patriarchs still stood. God always built on the foundation he had laid. The promises to David and Solomon were given to the descendants of the patriarchs, further specifying the Lord's purpose. With the call of the prophets God began a new stage in the preparation of his people. But he never abandoned what he did through Moses and later through David. He built on his earlier work. No promise made by the Lord to these his chosen ones was ever withdrawn.

The rejection of Saul for his disobedience did not involve the withdrawal of any divine promise. The only promise concerning Saul was that he would save the Israelites from the Philistines and their enemies round about (1 Samuel 9:16; 10:1). No promise was ever made to Saul about his descendants.

However, under the kings, the disobedience to God and his law multiplied. Unlike earlier periods, some of the leaders of God's people became the most rebellious. The evils under Solomon led to the schism between Judah and Israel, between the southern and northern kingdoms. Even now, the promises to Judah and Jerusalem were not withdrawn. Even though Judah possessed institutional legitimacy with the Davidic king, the temple and the chosen city of Jerusalem, God still sent his prophets to the "heretical" kingdom of the north, men like Amos and Hosea. Israel as well as Judah was still the recipient of the promise, even after the end of the northern kingdom (Ezekiel 37:19-28).

It is true that the realization of the promised blessings was dependent on the people's obedience to the Lord and the covenant (Deuteronomy 4 and 28). Terrible calamities will follow disobedience and apostasy. However, the Scriptures witness that God will not allow his purpose and his promise to be totally thwarted by human sin. We can sense in Scripture the problem posed to God by the extent of his people's infidelity. Through the inspiration of God's own Spirit we are given a glimpse of what appears as an anguished debate within God's own mind. How can he not destroy and punish so rebellious a people? But equally, how can his infinite love turn his back on those he has called and chosen? This inner divine conflict is shown to the prophet Hosea:

> My people are bent on turning away from me;
> so they are appointed to the yoke,
> and none shall remove it.
> How can I give you up, O Ephraim!
> How can I hand you over, O Israel!
> How can I make you like Admah!
> How can I treat you like Zeboiim!
> My heart recoils within me,
> my compassion grows warm and tender.
> I will not execute my fierce anger,
> I will not again destroy Ephraim;
> for I am God, and not man,
> the Holy One in your midst,
> and I will not come to destroy. (Hosea 11:7-9).

However, the Scriptures make clear that the promises were hardly ever fulfilled in the way that the recipients imagined. The destruction of Jerusalem and the exile of the Jews to Babylon were so traumatic because they seemed like a negation of the promises concerning their land and their people. We can sense this devastating shock in the Lamentations of Jeremiah:

> The Lord has become like an enemy,
> he has destroyed Israel;
> he has destroyed all its palaces,
> laid in ruins all its strongholds;
> and he has multiplied in the daughter of Judah
> mourning and lamentation.

He has broken down his booth like that of a garden,
laid in ruins the place of his appointed feasts;
the Lord has brought to an end in Zion
appointed feast and sabbath
and in his fierce indignation has spurned
king and priest. (Lamentations 2:5-6).

In fact, the Lord worked out the fulfillment of the promises in and through the disasters and calamities that befell his people. The promises were inherited and carried by a faithful remnant (Isaiah 10:20-22; 11:11-12; 37:31-32; Jeremiah 44:28; Ezekiel 6:8; Joel 2:32; Micah 2:12) who received the grace of repentance from the Lord. But even with the remnant, the fulfillment in the coming of the Messiah was not at all what they imagined.

The fulfillment exceeded the promises in both the manner in which they were fulfilled (what human mind could imagine in advance the crucifixion of the God-man?) and in the content (who could have imagined beforehand the call to share the eternal life of the Blessed Trinity?). Every single promise of the Lord is kept, the fulfillment necessarily being greater than any promise on its own appeared to offer. All the Messianic promises, which in the Old Testament seemed incompatible with one another, are fulfilled in Jesus Christ, who surpasses the concrete hopes of God's chosen people.

The New Testament. While many promises of the Old Testament are fulfilled with the first coming of the Messiah, other Old Testament promises will only reach fulfillment with the second coming of Jesus and the consummation of all things (e.g. Isaiah 2:4; 11:6-9). Moreover, Jesus himself makes promises concerning those who believe in him: "he who eats my flesh and drinks my blood has eternal life, and I will raise him up at the last day" (John 6:54); "I tell you, you are Peter, and on this rock I will build my church, and the powers of death shall not prevail against it" (Matthew 16:18); "I am with you always, to the close of the age" (Matthew 28:20). We can now examine how the principles concerning God's fidelity to the Old Covenant apply to the New Covenant in his Son.

First of all, while important lessons can be drawn from the Old Testament for the New, the parallel is not totally exact. The New Covenant is in principle everlasting. Jesus has become high priest for ever (Hebrews 6:20). In Jesus' blood, the union between God and man is declared eternal and unbreakable. This suggests that it is even more unthinkable that God would go back on his work through his Christian servants than that he would go back on his word and work through Abraham, Moses and David.

Secondly, during the Old Testament period and up to the whole life and ministry of Jesus, God was doing truly new things, though always building on what went before. Since the resurrection and ascension of Jesus, there can be no absolutely new thing. Everything is given in Jesus. So whatever appears to be quite new is only new to us either because we had lost it through our sin and disobedience or because the Spirit has later drawn out something implicit in the work of Jesus, like the outpouring of the Spirit on the Gentiles in Acts 10. Every "new thing" for Christians has the character of a restoration of something lost or an explicitation of the implicit.

Thirdly, the fulfillment of the New Testament promises is finally realized in the new heaven and the new earth. Full realization does not belong to this world that is passing away (1 Corinthians 7:31; Hebrews 11:16).

Application to the Churches

What application does all this have for the Lord's relationship to all the churches? Are the applications different for the ancient churches, the Orthodox and the Catholic, from the churches of the Reformation and those born of more recent revival movements in the nineteenth and twentieth centuries?

Evidently, it is as unthinkable that God would go back on his promises to the people of the New Covenant as that he would reject the people of the Old. Not only will God not reject his promises to his servants, but he will not deny their call and their work. Just as the Lord always acknowledges the witness of his Old Testament servants, Abraham, Moses and David, so he will always acknowledge the witness of his Christian servants, whether Peter and Paul, Athanasius and Augustine, Francis of Assisi and Thomas Aquinas, Martin Luther and John Calvin, John Wesley and Count von Zinzendorf, Dwight Moody and Charles Spurgeon. But the abiding witness of the Christian servants is primarily in heaven, only secondarily on earth. "Blessed indeed", says the Spirit, "that they may rest from their labors, for their deeds follow them" (Revelation 14:13).

But while God will never reject the witness of his servants, may he not reject the churches they influenced and fashioned? Each church tradition consists of people gathered by the Holy Spirit to belong to Jesus Christ, the Word made flesh. Each such church, whatever its form of ministry and government, represents people whose joining in faith has been sealed in the blood of Christ. It is he who has joined them. This fact is demonstrated in each church's celebration of the Lord's Supper, whatever their differences about the mode of the Lord's presence. Where a people has been joined by the Lord, where Jesus is the basis for their togetherness, he owns them as his own.

The ultimate distinctiveness of each Christian tradition is its particular witness to Jesus Christ. It is this witness that grounds its eternal validity. Its distinctive witness to Jesus is not simply its own achievement; it is the work of the Holy Spirit, for only those moved by the Holy Spirit can say, "Jesus is Lord" (1 Corinthians 12:3). The witness of each church is both their witness and the witness of the Holy Spirit (John 15:26-27). Because this witness is not simply their own, but the Spirit's, God is committed to it.

Every aspect of the Spirit's witness to Jesus, and concerning Jesus, has eternal value. It will stand forever in heaven. In this fundamental sense, the distinctive witness of each church will never pass away. Because it is the Spirit's role to reveal the things of Jesus (see Chapter Eight), it is the Spirit's will that each distinctive witness to Jesus be continued on earth. But the Spirit's thrust will also be to bring our separated witnesses into one. While we cannot guarantee that every detail of each church's witness will be preserved until the return of Jesus, we can be confident that the Lord will not allow any truly significant witness to his Son to be wholly lost through human sin.

That God will not abandon our churches does not mean that God will ensure their perpetuation along their present lines. God is committed to the witness to his Son, and to his glorification. He is committed to what he sees to be most basic to our churches. That may not always be what we think is most essential. There is no guarantee that present church institutions will always look the same. The unthinkable can happen for Christians, as it happened to the Jews. Our churches may suffer what look like major setbacks and calamities. Fierce persecution may ensue. The fall of Constantinople to the Moslems in 1453 must have been almost as traumatic for the Christians of the Byzantine Empire as the fall of Jerusalem was for the Jews.

However, the promises of the Lord still stand, as they stood for the Jewish exiles in Babylon. But the promises are worked out in the midst of divine punishment for our sins and the divine gift of repentance for our cleansing. Our unrepented sins and infidelities will not pass unpunished as we see from the warnings to the churches of Asia Minor (Revelation 2-3). We cannot treat the Lord and his cross with contempt, and not suffer the consequences. God is never indifferent to the sin of his people. But his faithfulness means that the gift of repentance will always be available, and he will never be without those who respond to this grace.

Non-denominationalism and Denominationalism in the Light of Scripture

From this survey of the Scriptural data about God's new moves and their relationship to the tradition, we can now draw some conclusions about the non-denominational and the denominational attitudes we find in different segments of the charismatic movement.

The Scriptures show that the historic Christian churches are right in their conviction that God does not turn his back on the past. The Lord does keep his promises. He will never abandon those who confess the name of his Son. However, they are wrong in every assumption that God is committed to all the details of the present structures of our churches. They are also wrong in every assumption that the Lord is not committed to other Christian traditions that they believe to be in error. Wherever there is a witness to Jesus Christ born of the Holy Spirit, to that the Lord is committed.

This analysis shows that the non-denominationals are right in their recognition that God can and does intervene in unexpected and unpredictable ways. There are decisive new eras in Christian history, even though there is now no additional content in what is revealed. They are right in refusing to tie God down to official patterns, and in affirming that the Lord is always sovereignly free to act through whomsoever he chooses, whether inside or outside the covenanted people. However they are wrong in their denial of the promises of God to the historic churches. They are wrong to reject those whom God has not rejected. They are wrong in any disdain for the Christian past.

A Third Way

We have been considering the inadequacies of the two obvious ways of relating the renewal to the churches, the non-denominational and the denominational. The non-denominational rejects the traditions, and seeks to build afresh from the New Testament, as though the intervening history had never happened. The denominational seeks to bring renewal to the church, but keeps one's own church at the center. The non-denominational makes an absolute of the present work of the Spirit, the denominational makes an absolute of the past. Each position seems very logical and reasonable to its supporters. But both fail to grapple successfully with the ecumenical grace at the heart of the renewal.

The ecumenism of the third way goes beyond occasional inter-church collaboration and occasional inter-church fellowship, because God has gone beyond these limited steps. The ecumenism of the third way goes beyond the willingness of some non-denominational charismatics to have fellowship with any brethren in Christ. But it also goes beyond the ecumenism of historic church people who see fellowship with other charismatics as something of a lower order than the communion enjoyed with members of one's own church.

The Lord is pointing us to a third way, the ecumenical way which truly recognizes and builds upon the ecumenical character of the renewal as a work of God. The third way will seek to do justice to both truths. It will recognize that the renewal as an ecumenical outpouring of God's grace is truly unprecedented, and that it cannot be submitted or subordinated to the life of any one church, however old and venerable. But it will also recognize that God does not go back on his work of the past. He will not abandon the Catholic and Orthodox churches any more than he refused to abandon Israel and Jerusalem. Nor will he abandon his later progeny in the churches of the Protestant Reformation, and those issuing from more recent revivals.

This third way is itself a new thing, unexplained and uncharted, precisely because the renewal is new. The churches do not know how to receive a fully ecumenical work of the Spirit. But the Spirit will teach those who humbly seek to know. Subsequent chapters will examine what is involved in living out this third way, by which alone the ecumenical grace of the renewal can bear its full fruit.

CHAPTER EIGHT

The Essential Work of the Holy Spirit

WE NEED THEN SOME CRITERIA FOR DETERMINING HOW THIS third way will work. How is it possible at one and the same time to be fully committed to the worldwide work of the Holy Spirit in and across all the Christian churches and to be fully committed as a loyal member of one's own church?

The best way to approach this question is to see what the New Testament says about the work and role of the Holy Spirit. There is one place in the Scriptures where there is a more systematic presentation of the work and activity of the Spirit of God. This is in the sixteenth chapter of John, where this teaching comes to us as the words of Jesus, instructing the disciples about the work of the Paraclete, the Counselor, who will come when Jesus "goes away." This teaching of Jesus on the work of the Holy Spirit is divided into two parts, which we may call the convicting and the revealing work of the Spirit. The convicting work concerns what we are to be saved from, the revealing work what we are being saved for.

The Spirit Convicts

"When he [the Counselor] comes, he will convince the world concerning sin and righteousness and judgment: concerning sin, because they do not believe in me; concerning righteousness, because I go to the Father, and you will see me no more; and concerning judgment, because the ruler of this world is judged" (John 16:8-11).

The Holy Spirit proves that the world is wrong about sin, righteousness and judgment. Insofar as the world still exists in Christians, they are convicted by the Holy Spirit of the sin of the world in them.

71

The Spirit Convicts re: Sin. The Holy Spirit reveals to each person that he/she is a sinner. The Spirit pierces our human defenses, breaks through all our walls of self-justification, by which we exonerate ourselves before God. When the Spirit comes, we can no longer behave like the Pharisee who lists his claims to God's favor (he fasts, he gives alms, he goes to "church"), and we are given the grace to say with the publican, "God, be merciful to me a sinner" (Luke 18:13).

Jesus' words in John 16 point especially to the faithlessness in all sin. We sin because we do not believe. This is not just a lack of religious faith in general, but a refusal to believe in Jesus, "because they do not believe in me" (John 16:9).

The Spirit Convicts re: Righteousness. The Holy Spirit makes clear our own unrighteousness, and manifests that the righteousness of God is found in Jesus. Jesus is the one who has died for our sins, who has paid the price on our behalf, and has become in his humanity the righteousness of God for us. As Paul tells the Romans, "in it [the gospel] the righteousness of God is revealed through faith for faith" (Romans 1:17; see also 3:21-22). Because Jesus has gone to the Father, his total union with the Father is declared. In heaven, at the Father's right hand, Jesus is "right" with God. In him, the human race is reconciled and made one with the Father. As Paul says Christ has been "made our wisdom, our righteousness and sanctification and redemption" (1 Corinthians 1:30).

Here the convicting and the revealing work of the Holy Spirit go together. As we see the righteousness of Jesus we see our own inherent unrighteousness. As we acknowledge our unrighteousness our eyes are opened to the righteousness of Jesus.

The Spirit Convicts re: Judgment. As sinners, we are subject to the judgment and wrath of God. But through the death of Jesus, which establishes his righteousness, the prince of this world, Satan, stands condemned. The text says that Satan is already judged (John 16:11). In other words, as we believe in the saving death of Jesus on the cross the Spirit of God convinces us interiorly that we are no longer condemned. "There is now no condemnation for those who are in Christ Jesus" (Romans 8:1). The grounds of accusation, our sins, have been removed. Satan, the accuser of the brethren, has no more basis on which to work. Freed from the clutches of Satan, in Christ we are free of divine judgment.

The Spirit Reveals

Immediately after the passage on the convicting work of the Spirit in John 16 comes the teaching of Jesus on the Spirit's revealing work:

> "When the Spirit of truth comes, he will guide you into all truth; for he will not speak on his own authority, but whatever he hears he will speak, and he will declare to you the things that are to come. He will glorify me, for he will take what is mine and declare it to you. All that the Father has is mine; therefore I said that he will take what is mine and declare it to you" (John 16:13-15).

As with the convicting work of the Spirit three revealing works of the Spirit are described: guidance into all truth; revealing what is to come; making known the things of Jesus. In a way similar to conviction concerning sin, righteousness and judgment, the three revealing activities of the Holy Spirit clearly overlap, but each phrase brings out something not spelled out by the other two.

The Spirit Guides into All Truth. Truth in John's gospel is not abstract, philosophical truth. It is the total harmony of being, complete consistency between the outer and the inner, full correspondence between thought and action. This is realized in Jesus, who comes from the Father, "full of grace and truth" (John 1:14).

Guidance into all truth then brings out important dimensions of the Spirit's work:

☐ Christians are led by the Spirit *into* this fulness; it is a movement, a process by which we are led into the fulness of truth

☐ this being led into all truth is a process of ever fuller participation in the life and mind of Jesus Christ; it is what Paul prays for when he writes, "that their hearts may be encouraged as they are knit together in love to have all the riches of assured understanding, and the knowledge of God's mystery of Christ, in whom are hid all the treasures of wisdom and knowledge" (Colossians 2:2-3).

The Spirit Reveals What Is Yet to Come. There is no doubt here an aspect of preparation for future trials, as happened with the revelation to Jesus about his passion and death, and as Paul was warned of his coming suffering ("the Holy Spirit warns me. . . . " Acts 20:23). However the *ta erchomena* (the things to come) are in their fulness the full blessings of the kingdom of God, the final completion of the work of the Messiah. This work of the Spirit is to reveal now something of what Paul writes about to the Ephesians:

"For he has made known to us in all wisdom and insight the mystery of his will, according to his purpose which he set forth in Christ as a plan for the fullness of time, to unite all things in him, things in heaven and things on earth" (Ephesians 1:9-10).

This is much more than knowing I am saved, much more than having a personal relationship with Jesus, essential though these are. It is to be drawn into the plan of God, to be given a vision of what we have been created for, so we can take hold of the inheritance lost through Adam's sin but restored to us through the cross of Christ.

The Spirit Takes from the Things of Christ and Makes Them Known to Us. The Spirit's revelation is totally concerned with Jesus Christ. Jesus does not say, "The Spirit will make me known" but, "He will take what is mine (*ek tou emou*) and declare it to you." The Spirit does not make known the person of Jesus in a way that is separated from his mission and his role in God's plan. The Spirit declares to us everything concerning Jesus: his person, his divine sonship, his work of redemption, his headship of the new creation, his full place in God's plan.

This inner revealing work of the Spirit then takes the objective Word written so many hundred years ago and makes it a living word, written on our inmost hearts (2 Corinthians 3:3). What was there objectively as a message from God to all now becomes subjectively in the believer a personal word to her/him, inscribed within in a way that transforms the mind and understanding.

Putting on the New Mind

The convicting and revealing work of the Holy Spirit raises the Christian's mind to the divine level. The Lord told the prophet, "As the heavens are higher than the earth, so are my ways higher than your ways and my thoughts than your thoughts." (Isaiah 55:9). The Holy Spirit overcomes this infinite gap, first in filling the human mind of Jesus with divine thoughts, and secondly by opening this divine knowledge to our human minds through union with the glorified humanity of Jesus.

As the Spirit convicts of sin, we are enabled to see sin as God sees it. No longer is sin simply a moral mistake. It is an horrendous personal affront to the majesty and holiness of God. Pope John Paul II has written powerfully in his recent letter on the Holy Spirit how the evil of sin can only be seen in relation to the cross: "Man does not know this dimension—he is absolutely ignorant of it apart from the Cross of Christ. So he cannot be convinced of it except by the Holy Spirit" (para. 32). That is, we can only understand the nature of sin and the wonder of its forgiveness by divine revelation.

Likewise, as the Spirit reveals the things of Christ and his place in the plan of God, so we are privileged to see these eternal realities as God himself sees them. Through many passages in Scripture, the Holy Spirit shows us how the Father sees the Incarnation of his beloved Son: in the revelation about divine wisdom (Proverbs 8:22-31); in the parable of the vineyard and the wicked tenants (Luke 20:9-18); in the prologue to John's gospel (John 1:1-18); in the kenosis hymn in Philippians (Philippians 2:5-11); in Paul's teaching in Colossians 1:15-20; in the introduction to Hebrews (Hebrews 1:1-4). All these and other passages open up to the humble seeker the mind of God centered on his Son, his glorious cross and resurrection. As we are interiorly enlightened by the Spirit from the Scriptures, we can say with the psalmist, "How precious to me are thy thoughts, O God!" (Psalm 139:17).

Thus Christians do not simply have a divine message preached to them by someone sent by God. God's own Spirit works inside the believer to raise the mind to this divine level. The receiver is raised to the level of the message. Our minds must be where God has called and placed us to be:

> "If then you have been raised with Christ, seek the things that are above, where Christ is, seated at the right hand of God. Set your minds on things that are above, not on things that are on earth. For you have died, and your life is hid with Christ in God" (Colossians 3:1-3)

God's plan is that our minds would be filled with his revelation so that we can judge all things from his perspective, i.e. in truth. As Christians, we have a divine standard by which to assess all things. This is not just an objective list of doctrines and moral principles, found in church creeds and statements of faith, but an internalized grasp of the divine reality and the divine plan written in us by the Holy Spirit.

Divine revelation in the Holy Spirit is not given to be an occasional boost or bonus, as if God just helps out our ignorance from time to time. No, revelation in the Spirit is intended as a normal element in the life of the Spirit. It is the way our spirits are created to function, to be receptacles for divine revelation.

However, revelation in the Spirit is the first part of a two-stage process. It is what God does. It is what the Spirit of God shows us. The second step is what we do with God's precious gift. We have to treasure these divine truths, making them the new basis for all our thinking. This is what Mary did, when she "kept all these things, pondering them in her heart" (Luke 2:19). This is what Paul calls "putting on the new mind." God gives us the power to cleanse our minds of the thinking of this world, and to replace it with his revealed truth. "Put off your old nature which belongs to your former manner of life and is corrupt through deceitful lusts, and be renewed in the spirit of your minds, and put on the new nature, created after the likeness of God in true righteousness and holiness" (Ephesians 4:22-24).

As we make the revealed truth of God the regular content of our minds, we are enabled to "think with God." This is to be a spiritual person, the true *pneumatikos*, who "judges all things, but is himself to be judged by no one" (1 Corinthians 2:15).

Thinking with God requires daily prayer. For only with daily prayer do we come regularly into God's presence, and attune ourselves to the divine wavelength. It requires daily feeding on God's Word, so that we are consciously saying: "I want to be fed by divine revelation. I want my mind shaped by the Word of God, not by the competing philosophies of the world." It demands daily self-examination and repentance, so that all the daily defilements of our minds are quickly cleansed by the blood of Jesus. It necessitates an expectant faith and an active mind, humbly seeking the enlightenment of God's Spirit.

Only as our minds are raised up to divine thinking can we know both the magnificence and the misery of the church. Through the Spirit, we can know the infinite wonder of the divine life that shapes the church, the true bride formed in heaven for the divine bridegroom. From this divine viewpoint, we can see how tragic is the deformity of the church, what dreadful wounds our sins and unbelief have inflicted on the intended bride, what horrible defilements these are in God's holy sight.

As a result our divisions no longer appear as quite natural forms of rivalry and competition, and our distinctive doctrines and practices no longer appear simply as badges of orthodoxy or heterodoxy, depending on our stance. No longer will the Word of God be able to say of us, "They have healed the wound of my people lightly, saying, 'Peace, peace', when there is no peace" (Jeremiah 6:14; 8:11).

We need not fear this purging gaze of the Lord. Even what is best in our traditions needs purification from our sinful biases and our possessive attitudes. "For no other foundation can any one lay than that which is laid, which is Jesus Christ. Now if any one builds on the foundation with gold, silver, precious stones, wood, hay, straw—each man's work will become manifest; for the Day will disclose it, because it will be revealed with fire, and the fire will test what sort of work each one has done" (1 Corinthians 3:11-13).

CHAPTER NINE

The Holy Spirit Confirms and Challenges

IN THE LAST CHAPTER, WE SAW HOW ON THE ONE HAND THE
Holy Spirit convicts the world in relation to sin, righteousness and
judgment and how on the other hand the same Spirit reveals the
things of God centered in Jesus Christ. The convicting and
revealing work of the Holy Spirit can be seen in the ways that the
Lord both challenges and confirms the churches through the
charismatic renewal. As the Spirit convicts the churches, so they
are challenged by the Lord. As the Spirit reveals Jesus and God's
plan of salvation centered on him, so the churches are confirmed
in the heart of their faith-profession.

As in John 16, the convicting and revealing roles of the Holy
Spirit are held together, so we can see both these roles in the
work of the Spirit in the churches today. However, holding them
in balance is not always easy. For example, many charismatics in
the historic churches experience the renewal in terms of confirming the heart of their church's faith, but they do not see to the
same degree how the Spirit is challenging their church to repentance and change. This may be because their loyalty blinds them
to their church's weaknesses and infidelities, or it may be a
tactical timidity that senses a need to prove their loyalty and get
accepted before making any challenge. On the other hand, many
other Christians truly touched by the Spirit are so conscious of
the low level of much denominational "life," so aware of the
immense gap between the ideals of the New Testament and what
they see in the historic churches, that they write the churches off
altogether. Restoration then becomes building from scratch,
leaving the ruins of the old churches to one side as incapable of

being re-built. This is to concentrate on the convicting work of the Spirit in a way that turns the conviction into a condemnation. As a result, the work of revelation is no longer confirmation of historic Christianity but a new construction.

In other words, the third way that avoids the opposites of denominationalism and non-denominationalism depends on holding in full balance the convicting and revealing works of the Holy Spirit. In terms of the work of God in charismatic renewal, this includes holding together the challenging and the confirming work of the Holy Spirit. Let us look more closely at what this involves in practice.

The Spirit Challenges

As the Spirit of God convicts the world of guilt in relation to sin, righteousness and judgment, so the Spirit's activity in the church uncovers every intrusion of world into church. Every way in which unbelief has infiltrated any Christian tradition will be exposed as unbelief by the coming of the Spirit of God. People baptized in the Spirit have all experienced this. Because they now believe in a deeper way, they see more clearly the faithlessness in their old life. They now see and suffer over the lack of faith manifested in so much church behavior. When you know that the Lord can and does speak to believers, you see the unbelief in attitudes that regard this as impossible. When you experience the Lord's intervention following prayer, you see the unbelief in all prayer that has no expectancy of divine action. When you preach in a way that seeks the leading of the risen Lord Jesus, you are conscious of the unbelief in all preaching that is simply coming out of the preacher's own resources. As you begin to submit your own plans to the Lord in faith, you get a glimpse of how the Lord is pained by all church procedures that allow him no space to act, how he is grieved by every agenda that has not been humbly submitted to his priorities. We will sense where the stark challenge of the prophets has relevance today: "An appalling and horrible thing has happened in the land: the prophets prophesy falsely, and the priests rule at their direction; my people love to have it so, but what will you do when the end comes?" (Jeremiah 5:30-31).

To emphasize the faith of charismatics is not to claim for them a spiritual superiority or a high degree of maturity. But it is to recognize that baptism in the Spirit is a deeper yielding in faith to the Lord Jesus. Many Christians who have been baptized in the Spirit are less stable and less wise than some who have not. But in the "baptism" they have surrendered control of their lives to Jesus Christ, and so they have experienced a quantum-leap in faith. And if they are faithful to the Lord's grace and learn to put on the new mind, the mind of Christ, they will acquire stability and wisdom from the Holy Spirit.

Another instance concerns consciousness of the work of Satan. People baptized in the Spirit become aware of the reality of Satan and evil spirits in a way that previously they were not. Like Jesus after his baptism, they experience the attacks of the accuser and the father of lies. It is as though it is not worth the enemy's effort to attack people openly until they have experienced the anointing of the Holy Spirit.

As a result of this anointing, Christians baptized in the Spirit are disturbed at the ways many church people and even some church leaders dismiss any talk of Satan and evil spirits as mythical and as the survival of pre-scientific ways of thinking. This blindness seems all the more extraordinary at a time when involvement in the occult is soaring, especially in Western Europe. Charismatics see this as another clear area where the Spirit summons the churches to repentance for their blindness and unbelief.

Precisely because the Holy Spirit reveals Jesus Christ, the Spirit's coming will work to expose and challenge every church formulation, practice and activity that is not centered on Jesus, the perfect image of the Father. Thus the Spirit will make Catholics uneasy, not about honoring Mary (Luke 1:48), but about all forms and expressions of Marian devotion that downplay or ignore the centrality of Jesus. Anything that obscures the uniqueness of Jesus' role as mediator between God and the human race will be contested by the Spirit. The Spirit will expose the ways in which Catholics have allowed the sacraments to obscure Jesus instead of revealing him. They will see the extent to which the sacraments have become "things" that in theory mediate the life of Jesus, but in effect have become ends in themselves. They will be convicted of ways in which explanation of the sacraments has replaced proclamation of Jesus' death and resurrection. They will be deeply saddened by the ways in which the great gifts of the Lord Jesus have been distorted by human sin and unbelief.

However, evangelical Protestants should expect that the same Holy Spirit of God will challenge them equally strongly. The Spirit will show them how they do something very similar with the Bible that Catholics have done with the sacraments. That is to make God's wonderful gift an end in itself. It is easier for us to cling to a ceremony or a text than it is to cling to the living God. In this way the Spirit will expose the fear that hearing the Lord in inner revelation will devalue the written Word of God. The Spirit will also challenge the individualism that has no vision for the upbuilding of the body of Christ. There is no Christian tradition that will not be deeply challenged by the ecumenical outpouring of the Spirit of God.

Moreover, there is no area of church life that will not be challenged. In coming upon believers individually and corporately the life-giving Spirit of God radically challenges every aspect of life: social, intellectual, familial, liturgical, educational, administrative. The Spirit challenges how we worship, how we serve, how we form fellowship, how we think, how we do theology, how we make decisions, how we deal with conflict.

The Spirit Confirms

The coming of the Holy Spirit in deep spiritual renewal is not merely disturbing, though if it were not disturbing, it would not be the Holy Spirit of God. The Spirit's coming is also profoundly encouraging for the believer. It is no misnomer for the Spirit to be called Paraclete (encourager, strengthener, consoler).

This confirming and strengthening role is directly associated with the revelation of Jesus and his kingdom. The Spirit will show those who are open to see that the heart of their church tradition is Jesus Christ. However weak and distorted the teaching and life of a particular church (local, national or international) may have become, the Spirit shows how its original *raison d'être* is Jesus Christ and a particular witness to him.

Every distinctive Christian tradition has a particular light on the person of Jesus and his work. The work of reconciliation in the Spirit is one of recovering the full revelation of the mystery of the incarnate Word of God. Thus Christians in liturgical traditions like the Anglican, the Catholic, the Lutheran and the Orthodox can find when they are baptized in the Spirit how their prayer-formulae express so richly the mystery of Christ. They suddenly see how the prayers of the eucharist are filled with thanksgiving and praise in a way they had never noticed before. The Trinitarian structure of the liturgy may strike them with new force. The role of Jesus as great high priest may stand out in a new way.

Lutherans baptized in the Spirit will find their basic belief in justification by faith confirmed and given new life. They will realize with new clarity how impossible it is for fallen human beings to gain acceptance by God on the basis of anything originating in themselves. Methodists will appreciate with new depth John Wesley's passion for the lost, his commitment to evangelism and his concern to bring all converts into a network of classes for pastoral care and formation. Calvinists will find the Spirit confirming the total sovereignty of God. Christians like Baptists and Mennonites will find a confirmation of their understanding of the local church gathered by Jesus Christ.

Finding the Center

This confirming work of the Spirit of God illuminates the core or center of the faith of each tradition. From being a people who perhaps believed in a list of doctrines or those who had distinctive theological emphases, we become believers with new clarity on the centrality of Jesus Christ. We see how the Incarnation is the climax of salvation history and Jesus' passion and death on the cross is the climax of his human life, leading to his glorious resurrection and ascension into heaven.

Before, we may have known intellectually that Jesus was the center, but now it is lit up within us. Other aspects of Christian faith are necessarily subordinated to this illuminated center. Our particular denominational emphases become less absolute and less independent as they are set more firmly in the light of Jesus Christ.

Not everything becomes crystal clear immediately when we discover this center of our faith. But when we know the center, we know that all else has to be reviewed and re-thought in the light of that center. We have light on the center, but that light has to grow, for in Christ "are hid all the treasures of wisdom and knowledge" (Colossians 2:3). As that light grows, we will see more clearly how to evaluate all other aspects of our inherited faith.

This rediscovered center is the point of our new-found unity in the Spirit. For the Christ who is center of my tradition is the same Christ who is center of yours. That is why the unity of those baptized in the Spirit is a deep spiritual reality, not just an emotional feeling of oneness.

The Balance of the Third Way

It is already clear that the third way avoiding denominationalism and non-denominationalism involves holding together the challenging and the confirming work of the Holy Spirit. This holding together can be described as a matter of balance. It is certainly not compromise. It is the balance of the Spirit, not the balance of fallen human reason.

It is not that the Holy Spirit fully confirms one set of truths or practices such as the Trinity, the Incarnation, the eucharist, justification by faith, the role of Mary, baptism-conversion, and then challenges other areas seen simply as errors. While the Spirit confirms what is at the heart of all these things, the Spirit also challenges the ways we have held these same truths, the limitations we have introduced, the narrowing down from Scriptural richness to denominational or confessional rigidity. The work of challenging and the work of confirmation are then virtually inseparable. We can only attain the balance by prayerful submission to the fulness of divine revelation, not by any kind of negotiated trade-off.

CHAPTER TEN

Ecumenical Gift and Challenge

THE OUTPOURING OF THE HOLY SPIRIT BOTH CHALLENGES every Christian church, summoning it to repentance, and confirms the heart of each Christian tradition as being Jesus Christ, the one Savior and Lord of all. However, the Spirit does not only challenge each church separately, so that Anglicans are being confronted by the heart of the gospel here, Catholics there, Lutherans somewhere else, Presbyterians in yet another place, etc. It is not that Lutheran charismatic renewal confirms and challenges the Lutheran Churches, the Catholic renewal the Roman Catholic Church, the Anglican renewal the churches of the Anglican Communion, etc. Naturally, the challenge to each church has to come first through the members of that church touched by the Spirit of God. But the challenge to each church comes primarily from the "naked grace" common to this work of the Spirit in all the churches.

The evidence presented in earlier chapters shows that this renewal in the Holy Spirit is at its heart an ecumenical grace of God poured out on all the churches. The grace given is not different from one church to another. What is different are the varied traditions into which this grace is being received. This means that the grace given is in a vital sense more than what any church tradition now "possesses." We can glimpse perhaps how God in his infinite wisdom saw that only a grace transcending the present endowments of the churches could be a grace for all equally, and only such a transcendent ecumenical grace could summon and bring the divided churches into unity.

This ecumenical grace, containing something more than each tradition now knows in separation, adds an extra dimension to the challenging and confirming work of the Holy Spirit. Through the baptism in the Holy Spirit the Lord is not only confirming the heart of each Christian tradition, but he is restoring the fulness of our Christian heritage. He is reversing the narrowing process involved in the schisms and divisions of the centuries. In other words, the ecumenical grace of the renewal invites each tradition, not only to rediscover its own core or center, but also to open itself to things that have been lost or ignored down the ages.

This opening up to what may initially seem alien to one's own church tradition has two distinct aspects. The first is an opening up to what the Lord confirms in traditions other than our own. The second is an opening up to what has been lost or forgotten by all the historic churches.

It is vital that Christians in all church traditions are open to the Spirit's work of recovery and restoration. There will be a tendency on the part of fallen human nature either to reject out of hand what is wholly unfamiliar or to say that we have had it all along. So church people can use unfamiliarity with such practices as the spiritual gifts and spontaneous vocal praise as a reason for rejecting this work of the Spirit. Or those who accept them can try to prove that their tradition has known such things all along, not really facing up to the newness in what the Spirit is doing.

There is a basic difference here between this challenge as it comes to the traditions of more recent centuries, which stemmed from protests and efforts at reform (in some cases of efforts at restoration) and the oldest traditions of the Catholics, the Orthodox and the other ancient churches of the East, which historically precede all movements of reform and restoration. In general, it is much easier to tell if some reality, teaching or practice, has ever been part of the more recent traditions. They are more recent, so there is less history to learn from. Being born of reform their distinctive tenets and practices are simpler and their church tradition is less complex and less cluttered. The complexity of the older church traditions is at one and the same time a grace and a hazard. It means there is a richness of spiritual inheritance, a wealth of spiritual wisdom to sift and treasure. But it also means that there is difficulty in seeing the wood for the trees. The arteries may be clogged and so the heart itself may be obscured.

For the Reformed Christian, openness to the forgotten or unknown means opening out from their distinctive Reformation emphases. It means looking beyond the central truths on which the Reformers took their stand (justification by faith, the sufficiency of the Scriptures, the absolute sovereignty of God) to the full plan of God revealed in his Word (the new creation, the church as the body of Christ, the reconciliation of all things under Christ's headship). For the Catholic or Orthodox Christian, it means clarifying the center, bringing basic truths to their rightful centrality, throwing light from the center on the periphery. It means uncluttering the inheritance.

We have already singled out revelation in the Spirit as one of the hallmarks of this renewal. There is a directness in God's self-communication and activity that has not been known as part of ordinary Christian life in any of the major traditions in recent times. Here the ecumenical grace of the charismatic renewal challenges all churches equally.

The Holy Spirit's action uncovers our inherited fears of "the other," the Catholic fear of everything Protestant, the Protestant fear of Rome, the Eastern suspicion of the West, Western suspicion of the East. Let us now look at ways in which the Holy Spirit is urging us to overcome the fears and suspicions of centuries. Let us see how the Holy Spirit is leading us to receive again as our common Christian heritage the truths and realities that have been restricted to particular Christian churches for so long.

Salvation through the Blood of Jesus

Talk about salvation through the blood of Jesus strikes most Catholics as being very Protestant. In fact, it is not only characteristic of evangelical Protestantism, it is scriptural, and it has been the faith of Christians throughout the history of the church.

The Holy Spirit makes Christians value the blood of Jesus. The Spirit convicts us of sin, not just of our personal acts of disobedience to God, but that of ourselves we are totally incapable of bridging the chasm sin has opened between us and God. The Spirit reveals that it is only by the blood of Jesus that our sins are removed, that we are reconciled to the Father and made clean.

The Holy Spirit makes clear to the Christian mind that this is the only way to deal with sin. God's answer to sin is repentance and faith in the saving power of Jesus' blood. Other ways of tackling evil do not eliminate it. Only the blood of Jesus has the power to reach within the sinner to cleanse the conscience, to change inner dispositions and to remove all guilt.

Catholics need to overcome their fear of biblical language. In fact, there is much in Catholic devotional history about the blood of Jesus, as can be seen, for example, in the writings of St. Catherine of Siena (1347-1380) and St. Alphonsus Liguori, the founder of the Redemptorists (1696-1787). This is a foundational truth to which contemporary Catholicism urgently needs to be recalled. Today's Catholics hear very little about sin and repentance. Often the roots of sin are simply being massaged by psychological methods of counseling that fail to mention repentance and the blood of Jesus. Let Catholic readers ask God's forgiveness for the ways they have ignored and spurned the precious blood of his Son by turning elsewhere to deal with sin.

Dying to Sin through the Cross of Jesus

Similarly, talk of the cross as the instrument of the Holy Spirit to deal with the flesh of the believer will strike most Catholics as rather Protestant. In fact, it is a vital biblical truth known in those Protestant circles, particularly influenced by the teaching of the Keswick movement at the beginning of this century.

For the repentant Christian, the Holy Spirit brings to life the teaching of Paul on the cross as the instrument by which the flesh is put to death. The flesh represents those drives and tendencies in fallen human nature which are not under God's authority and which if unchecked pull us into sin. Paul speaks of this power, our flesh, being crucified and put to death at the cross. He cries out, "Those who belong to Christ Jesus have crucified the flesh with its passions and desires" (Galatians 5:24).

In other words, the cross of Jesus is the only instrument capable of putting to death our cravings for sin, our itch to rebel, our desires for independence from God. When temptations assail the mind, it is only as the believer turns to the cross in faith and proclaims the power of Christ over these desires that they can be killed off and their power annulled. It is to claim in each situation of struggle the fundamental grace of baptism, to be dead with Christ. Believing that we have died with Christ (Colossians 3:3), we can put to death by the cross the remaining manifestations of the power of sin (Colossians 3:5).

When the Holy Spirit brings this knowledge of the power of the cross of Christ, real and lasting victory over sin becomes possible. The axe is then laid to the root of the tree. Rediscovery of the power of the cross is clearly one of the most important revelatory works of the Holy Spirit.

Though this understanding of the cross is not well-known among contemporary Catholics, it is in fact expressed in the well-known hymn of Cardinal Newman, *Firmly I believe and truly*:

> And I trust and hope most fully
> In that manhood crucified;
> And each thought and deed unruly
> Do to death, as he has died.

Faith Actions in the Name of Jesus

One of the Protestant fears the Holy Spirit desires to remove is the suspicion of ritual, in particular the instinctive opposition to anything implying that God uses gestures to confer his grace. Yes, Jesus does reject merely quantitative repetition (Matthew 6:7), but it is also clear that his gestures are expressions of his total trust in the Father, and that these gestures are instrumental in people's healing and forgiveness (Mark 1:41; 5:41; 8:23, 25).

The Protestant fear of attributing any causality to the act of baptizing in water is itself unscriptural. This is not to approve all Catholic mentalities regarding baptismal practice, but the Holy Spirit is convicting them of different things. The comparison of circumcision with baptism in Colossians 2:11 clearly points to a causative action in faith, an interpretation confirmed by Peter: "Baptism . . . now saves you, not as a removal of dirt from the body, but as an appeal to God for a clear conscience, through the resurrection of Jesus Christ" (1 Peter 3:21).

The restoration of the spiritual gifts has helped to bring home the power of God in faith-filled actions performed by the Christian: in laying hands on the sick, in anointing, in commissioning for ministry, all of which have clear scriptural precedent.

Authority and the Body of Christ

Another Protestant fear the Holy Spirit attacks is the fear of authority, and of any believers submitting their wills to anyone except God and Jesus. It is understandable that Christians have reacted to abuses of authority by resisting all ideas of submission within the church. But it is not scriptural. The New Testament tells us: "respect those who labor among you and are over you in the Lord and admonish you" (1 Thessalonians 5:12) and "Be subject to one another out of reverence for Christ" (Ephesians 5:21).

The experience of people baptized in the Holy Spirit is that spiritual gifts are given for the sake of the body of Christ (1 Corinthians 12). Experience with the gifts shows how the gifted Christians have to submit the exercise of those gifts to other gifted persons within the body of Christ. As Paul says, "the spirits of prophets are subject to prophets. For God is not a God of confusion but of peace" (1 Corinthians 14:32-33).

The experience of the renewal thus emphasizes the need for spiritual authority. It reveals the living body of Christ as the goal of the Spirit, a body in which all are "members one of another" (Romans 12:5; Ephesians 4:25). The Holy Spirit convicts all, Protestant and Catholic, of our pervasive individualism, summoning us beyond merely human views of individual maturity to see the perfect Christian as one who is fully integrated with other Christians into the body of Christ (Ephesians 4:13). The Holy Spirit never simply tells us to copy the practice of other churches. The Spirit desires to teach us all from the fulness of God's revelation in Christ. Freedom from fears means being set free from inherited prejudice so we can hear the full Word of God.

These examples concern the mutual fears of Catholics and Protestants. Similar points could be made in regard to the Catholic-Protestant West and the Orthodox East. But usually the Lord starts his work of healing and reconciliation with those nearest home.

Call to Deeper Renewal

The convictions given in these examples are not equally widespread throughout the charismatic renewal. For the renewal is primarily an events-movement that has to seek out its significance. It does not come with a ready-made set of teachings. However, as with all movements of the Holy Spirit, there is a powerful thrust in the renewal to base Christian life on the Scriptures as the inspired Word of God. As those filled with the Spirit seek their nourishment in the Scriptures, the Spirit brings to life passages whose meaning has lain hidden or neglected for many Christians.

In the maturest segments of the renewal movement, we can see the fuller embodiment of these biblical teachings. These make plain the direct link between maturity in the Spirit and ecumenical openness. For it is as Catholics have been open to truths more known among Protestants, and Protestants have been open to truths more known among Catholics that a fuller richness emerges. Our heritage is further expanded by all the Lord has to teach us from the Orthodox East and from what Messianic Judaism brings us from a deeper grasp of the Old Covenant. The result is a greater fulness of divine revelation among God's people.

CHAPTER ELEVEN

Ecumenical Grace Requires Ecumenical Response

THE THIRD WAY BY WHICH THE HOLY SPIRIT RENEWS THE people of God and thereby brings them into unity neither writes off the churches as they are nor absolutizes them. This chapter will spell out two complementary principles which are essential to this third ecumenical way: (1) all church traditions need this Holy Spirit renewal; (2) this Holy Spirit renewal needs all the church traditions.

Each need involves an element of submission. The churches need to submit themselves to this contemporary action of the Holy Spirit, so that they can be purified and raised up to new life by the Lord. The emerging renewal in its turn needs to submit itself to the traditions of the churches, so that no aspect of God's Word is forgotten and unheeded. Together these two patterns of mutual submission involve a surrender to the full revelation of God, mediated by the totality of his Word. Failure in either of these tasks results in a narrowing distortion of the Christian message.

The Development of the Movement in the Churches

When this work of the Holy Spirit began in the churches, it had the character of a "naked grace." That is to say, it did not begin as an organized system, as a coherent plan, as something "ready-made" with its own theories and self-understanding. It began, as we have seen, more as an "event" than as an "idea." Something began to happen, and only then did questions of meaning arise. As people were touched by the Lord, as believers began to hear the Lord in a new way and to experience his power in their lives, they were faced with two questions (1) What does it mean? (2) What do we do with it?

Both these questions raise the issue of church. Both face participants with the question: "How does this work of God relate to our understanding of church?" For Christians convinced of the importance of their church and its tradition in God's plan, the question becomes more concrete: "How should this relate to our church?" These Christians will naturally want to bring this work of the Spirit into the heart of their church. They see that the convincing-revealing work of the Holy Spirit is needed by their church if it is to be renewed.

For a church to be renewed, all dimensions of its life need to be exposed to the challenge of the Spirit: worship, theology, education, pastoral practice, evangelism, service to the poor and oppressed, administration. However to be true to the grace of the Lord, it is vital that we are clear on *what* is being brought into the heart of the church. That is why it is so important that the more basic question "What does it mean?" be answered before the practical question "What should we do with it?" One big temptation has been to assume that the answer to the first question was obvious, and to rush to get on with the second. For example, people could say: it is obvious what it means, it is the power of the Holy Spirit for the life of the church. So we go ahead and organize on that basis. The problem here is that people's previous understanding of church controls their subsequent decisions. Then as the movement necessarily develops from its initial and unformed explosion of life and power to take on organizational shape, it will inevitably be fitted into our old ways of thinking and acting.

If baptized in the Spirit Christians from each church tradition organize and develop the renewal in accordance with their received ideas of church, ministry, and mission, then what began as one ecumenical move of God will end back where we started. It will mean each church has tried to harness God's life and power for its own purposes. The only way to avoid this tragedy is to recognize that all church traditions are being called upon to surrender themselves in trusting faith to the one God, whose Spirit is being poured out afresh.

Understanding the Renewal as an Ecumenical Work of God

We can only respond properly to this work of the Lord as we understand what it is. For this, we need the light of the Holy Spirit (see Chapter Six). A fundamental element in this understanding is that the renewal is in its essence an ecumenical grace for all the churches and for all Christians.

This fact provides us with a key principle: an ecumenical grace of God can only be understood ecumenically. It is right and proper that in seeking understanding we should turn first to the resources of our own tradition. Among Catholics, this will mean the resources of the Catholic Church in communion with Rome. For evangelicals, it may mean the resources of evangelical Protestant tradition more than the tradition of any one denomination. However, the more we try to understand and shape the renewal according to the received ideas and emphases of only one tradition, the more we will find that these resources are not adequate to the task, i.e. it does not work. There is something radically unsatisfactory about trying to fit something inherently ecumenical, as wide as the full gospel revelation of God, into our reduced denominational containers.

This does not mean that there is no gospel in our churches and their traditions. Rather there is a constant tension between the gospel and life of God in our churches and the structures and framework that contain it. It is precisely the convicting and challenging work of the Holy Spirit mentioned in Chapters Eight and Nine that confronts the structures and framework (all our theological categories, all our administrative patterns) with the need to expand them to the breadth, the height, the length and the depth of the gospel of Christ.

The inadequacy of everybody's received categories can be seen in many presentations of baptism in the Spirit, the central grace of the charismatic renewal. Catholics are worried about appearing to ignore or downgrade church teaching on the sacraments of baptism and confirmation. So they often describe baptism in the Spirit as the release and coming to conscious awareness of the graces objectively conferred in baptism and confirmation. But this does not really explain anything. It is not allowing the Holy Spirit to open up a fuller understanding of baptism and Christian initiation. It is not a reflection on what has happened to people baptized in the Spirit. Such a reflection would give a prominent place to the Word of God and to the faith of the believer. However, most evangelical Protestant presentations are not much better. Their concern has been not to undermine their traditional understanding of receiving the Holy Spirit in conversion and regeneration, and of knowing Jesus personally in that event. As a result, baptism in the Spirit tends to be understood in terms of power for mission. This kind of concern then leads either to a separation of the Son known in conversion from the Spirit received at the baptism or to a coming of the Spirit in the baptism that does not affect the believer's relationship to the Father and the Son.

Both these inadequate views of baptism in the Spirit result from trying to explain this reality in terms of inherited categories. Both pay more attention to traditional formulations than they do to what has actually happened to people in the renewal.

It is one of the results of division among Christians that the infinitely rich treasure of divine revelation, the full mystery of Christ, has become sundered and distorted. As a result, some facets of the gospel and mystery of Jesus are more strongly grasped in one tradition, other aspects in another tradition, and still others in others. The consequence is that God's outpoured grace for the renewal and reunion of his people can only be grasped and received ecumenically. Catholics cannot understand it fully in received Catholic categories, nor can they fit it completely into existing Catholic structures. The same applies to Lutherans, to Anglicans, to evangelical Protestants, etc.

The reception and understanding of this ecumenical grace has to be done by all together. Naturally Catholics will bring their inherited categories with all their advantages and disadvantages, with their mixture of deep spiritual wisdom and of cramping rigidity. Lutherans will bring their resources, which too will be a mixture of divine gift and of human limitations. The same will be true of every authentic Christian tradition that confesses the name of Jesus as Savior and Lord.

The different traditions do not each bring the same percentage of treasure. In general, the older traditions bring more, both more treasure and more dross. But it is futile to argue about percentages. The two per cent brought by one smaller tradition may be like the widow's mite. It is every bit as much part of the Lord's gift to all his people, as the larger treasures of Rome, Constantinople, Wittenberg, Canterbury and Geneva.

The parts of the other traditions that are from the Lord will then correct and challenge the dross in our own. Catholic clericalism will be challenged by the Holy Spirit's work activating the priesthood of all believers among Protestants. Evangelical logic will be challenged by the Holy Spirit's work in liturgical traditions, holding together apparent opposites in the one mystery of Christ. Catholic neglect of the Scriptures will come under the hammer of the Spirit, while Anglican comprehensiveness will be tested in the fire of divine fulness. The rightness in Luther's teaching on word and sacrament will be enriched by a fuller light on the mutual coinherence of the persons of the Trinity.

What about Doctrinal Conflict?

Experience in the renewal confirms what should be obvious. Not all our doctrinal barriers and misunderstandings are going to dissolve overnight. Protestant charismatics are not going to find their difficulties with the Mass and Mary instantly dissolved. Catholics are not suddenly going to find it any easier to understand the Protestant individualism that has little place for the church as the communion of saints.

One result of being brought together by the Holy Spirit, and being touched by God in an identical way, is to love, trust and respect the work of God in each other. We then know that these are truly our brothers and sisters in Jesus Christ. Even though they still believe in and do things we have problems with, we are even more certain that the Spirit of God is in them glorifying Jesus than we are about the things that divide us.

However, this confidence depends on the renewal being faithful to its ecumenical origins. We can only retain the trust of our brothers and sisters in the Spirit in other churches when they know we are sincerely seeking the fulness of God's revelation, and when they know we are submitting our tradition to the Holy Spirit, as the Spirit opens up the Word of God. They can only retain our trust as we know they are doing the same in their own tradition. This trust and confidence require a building on the ecumenical contacts and bridges established by the Spirit in the early years.

The Renewal Needs the Traditions

In the first enthusiasm of charismatic fervor, it is easy to see that the churches need this grace of the Spirit. It is probably less easy to see that this move of the Spirit needs the churches and their traditions.

We can perhaps see this need more clearly if we look at what typically happens when a new church or denomination springs up as a result of the forcefulness and the distinctive teaching of its leader. In that situation, the new group is typically limited by the limitations of the founder. Elements in the Scriptures that did not impinge on the founder have little or no place in the new denomination. It is in a real sense conceived in the image and likeness of the founder. It is like Seth being conceived in the image and likeness of Adam (Genesis 5:3), where Adam had been created in the image of God (Genesis 1:27). Sometimes these founders have been men of great sanctity and depth: John Wesley, who in any case didn't intend to found a new denomination, is an obvious example. However, even with the greatest merely human founder, and of course a fortiori with those of lesser stature, the resulting tradition will be less than catholic. That is to say, it will reflect important aspects of Christian revelation (it may like the Wesleyan movement perform a marvellous and much needed work of God in a particular generation), but it will be lacking in a wholeness. The work of Christian reunion is the restoration of that wholeness, that the one body of Christ may manifest the fullness of divine revelation.

We cannot exclude the possibility of God raising up leaders outside the historic churches to bear witness to aspects of the gospel to which these churches are closed. But even then, these new churches can never on their own know the fulness of the mystery of Christ. The day will come when the old churches are open again to receive this witness. The old need the new, and the new need the old.

Each church tradition, whether old or new, has to subordinate itself to the heart of the gospel revealed by the Spirit through the Scriptures. So does each new outpouring of the Spirit. This submission to the heart of the gospel also involves a submission to the heart of all Christian traditions, by which the understanding of the gospel has been handed down.

As initially a "naked grace" as yet fluid, unformed and unorganized, the renewal has to become embodied, not as a church in itself but in the life of the churches. Insofar as the charismatic renewal is now an organized movement in the churches, it needs input and correction from the historic church traditions.

The renewal needs this input first of all to assure its catholicity and to avoid becoming a narrow movement living off a reduced segment of the full revelation in Christ. As the renewal develops, it needs to test itself against the fulness of the mystery of Christ, mediated through the totality of the Scriptures. This fulness has been transmitted through the traditions of the churches, even though it has become fragmented through their divisions. The fulness being fragmented, the yardstick of measurement now needs to take account of the work of God in all the Christian traditions.

Tom Smail's book *The Forgotten Father* is an example of this kind of corrective. Smail saw that in much of the charismatic renewal there was more mention of the Son and the Spirit than of the Father. That this was an imbalance needing correction can be seen from the Scriptures, as they have been lived and understood in the historic church traditions.

The need for the renewal to submit itself to the traditions of the churches so as to assure its catholicity applies particularly to its measuring itself against the breadth and the wealth of the oldest Christian traditions. However the renewal does not only need to measure itself against such ancient traditions as the Catholic and the Orthodox, but also against the later traditions that arose out of protest and reform. Here the test is whether the renewal as it takes shape is doing justice to their central insights. Is it recognizing the importance of the Lutheran conviction about justification by faith? Is it recognizing the importance of the local church and the priesthood of all believers so dear to Congregationalists, Baptists and Mennonites?

Here too the ecumenical dimension is vital. If it is only Catholic charismatics who are strong on sacraments and authority, only Lutheran charismatics who are strong on justification by faith, and only evangelical charismatics who affirm the importance of adult conversion, then again the development of the movement would be leading from ecumenical beginnings back into the denominational compartments from which we came.

The truths of God embedded in each tradition are meant to belong together. Charismatics constantly find themselves fed by truths coming out of traditions other than their own. Of course, not everything in this inter-church market is healthy and of the Lord, and discernment is needed. But this cross-pollination is basically right, and it belongs to the nature of what God is doing. As the Anglican John Gunstone has said recently, "It is one of the strange results of the charismatic movement that the inspirations of one particular Christian tradition are often rediscovered by those nurtured in another."

The submission of the renewal to the churches is not simply the renewal saying to the churches: "You tell us what to do, and we'll do it." It is a matter of everyone yielding to the Holy Spirit manifesting the Lordship of Christ. This means the churches as they are accepting the challenge of the Spirit. It means those in the renewal submitting themselves to the richness of God mediated through the churches. This process of mutual submission (of the churches to the Holy Spirit manifest in the renewal and of the renewal to the Holy Spirit present in the churches and their traditions) will lead to a sifting of the real Tradition from the limiting and distorting elements in their particular traditions.

An ecumenical grace calls for ecumenical implementation. Ecumenical implementation is impossible without ecumenical understanding. In other words, an ecumenical grace calls for an ecumenical theology. Anything less will distort the gift of God, and thwart the fulfillment of God's purpose.

CHAPTER TWELVE

Overcoming the Biggest Dangers

WE ARE NOW IN A POSITION TO IDENTIFY THE BIGGEST DAN-
gers standing in the way of this ecumenical grace of the renewal in
the Spirit producing its full fruit in all the churches.

All danger to God's saving grace comes from sin. The only
obstacle to God's sovereign love is in the hardness of human
hearts, reinforced by the power of Satan. Whenever God pours
out his love and mercy on fallen creation, there is resistance and
conflict. We see this supremely in the Incarnation, "He came to
his own home, and his own people received him not" (John 1:11).

In our fallen condition, we have chosen to live and organize the
world independently of God. That was the choice of Adam and
Eve, when they preferred the word of the serpent to the Word of
God. It is the choice which all subsequent generations have made
their own. We have centered our lives on ourselves, our families,
our tribes and our nations instead of on God and his will. God's
messengers do not receive an automatic welcome in this alien-
ated world. Jesus knew this when he told the parable of the
wicked tenants. After beating, maiming or killing the servants
sent by the owner of the vineyard, "He had still one other, a
beloved son; finally he sent him to them, saying, 'They will
respect my son.' But those tenants said to one another, 'This is
the heir; come, let us kill him, and the inheritance will be ours.'
And they took him and killed him, and cast him out of the
vineyard" (Mark 12:6-8).

Christian faith has always affirmed that salvation has only come
to us through a death, the death of Christ. For us to receive the
grace of God, there has to be a death in us as well. We have to die
to the flesh, to the way of life centered on ourselves, our appe-

tites, our ambitions, our schemes. We can only die to the flesh by being inserted into the saving death of Jesus. This happens by faith and baptism. "Do you not know that all of us who have been baptized into Christ Jesus were baptized into his death? (Romans 6:3).

The dangers preventing this ecumenical grace from realizing its God-given potential are all forms of refusal to die. Obviously, the first danger is outright refusal to recognize this movement as a work of the Spirit of God, either by attributing it to evil spirits, as often happened at the start of the Pentecostal movement, or by dismissing it as merely the product of socio-cultural circumstances. However, the biggest dangers probably come from within, from those who accept something of this grace, but do not want to die to the flesh, or do not see the need for it. Let us look at some of the ways in which this can happen.

Fleshly Renewal

As a "naked grace" poured upon the churches without a ready-made system and without an accompanying self-understanding, the renewal in the Holy Spirit did not come in a definite shape with clear-cut goals and priorities. The "naked grace" had to be clothed. That is to say, participants have had the opportunity and the responsibility to shape the movement. As we have stressed, faithful shaping of this work of God depends on receiving understanding of its significance from the Holy Spirit.

Fleshly renewal sees no need for such understanding. Fleshly renewal places the emphasis on emotions and feelings. It would see baptism in the Spirit as not so much a mysterious work of God to be reverenced and understood, but a marvelous experience to be enjoyed. While the baptism in the Holy Spirit is often accompanied by intense joy, fleshly renewal is unable to distinguish between the rejoicing of the spirit and excitement of the soul, that is simply the arousal of emotions and feelings.

Where there is an element of flesh in renewal, there remains a degree of self. Whereas before conversion people sought happiness in the world, now they seek happiness through Jesus. But where the flesh is operative, the focus is more on their own happiness than on the Lord. Fleshly renewal can be so insidious because people can appear to be so joyful and excited by the Lord. But where the flesh rather than the spirit is the principle of our behavior, then the rejoicing has slipped from being delight in the Lord to being delight in our own feelings about the Lord. This is wrong because God is being used to serve self, instead of the self being crucified so the new life can serve God.

The key question is whether people are open to the Spirit moving them on from excitement over their experience of the Lord to simple love of the Lord himself. This is the shift from an immature focus on self and dependence on emotions to a mature love of God for who he is. This objective love of God is marvelously portrayed by the prophet Habakkuk:

> Though the fig trees do not blossom, nor fruit be on the vines, the produce of the olive fail and the fields yield no food, the flock be cut off from the fold and there be no herd in the stalls, yet I will rejoice in the Lord, I will joy in the God of my salvation (Habakkuk 3:17-18).

One major test of willingness to grow out of fleshly immaturity is our openness to being convicted of sin and to being brought to repentance. The fleshly Christian may be tempted to dismiss all calls to repentance as negative reversions to pre-pentecostal gloom. Pentecost can be far more attractive than Calvary. It is always a danger sign when people talk constantly of Pentecost, but rarely of the cross of Calvary.

Where there is no regular repentance for sin, and no conscious dying to old ways of thinking, any "renewal" is superficial and ultimately illusory. An outward charismatic style of joy and enthusiasm covers over all the old patterns which remain largely unchanged beneath the surface. That is why this kind of "joy" is always somewhat frenetic, anxious and clinging.

Fleshly renewal means using the Holy Spirit of God for our own ends. For example, wanting to be healed so I can do what I want to do, rather than wanting healing so I can serve and glorify the Lord; rejoicing in the baptism in the Spirit primarily because it has made me a more likeable person, and things prosper instead of going wrong.

Fleshly renewal does not mean that such people were never truly touched by the Holy Spirit. It means that for whatever reason (often a lack of sound teaching and wise leadership) the Holy Spirit has subsequently been subordinated to people's old ways, especially subservience to their emotions, instead of their old ways being brought to the cross and the Holy Spirit bringing forth the new creation of the resurrection, the full fruit of the Spirit.

Those of us in the renewal need to repent for the ways we have shared in and been responsible for fleshly renewal. Fleshly renewal is one of Satan's main ways of neutralizing this work of the Spirit. It is so serious because it is a counter-witness to the churches. It is a major obstacle to open and sensitive Christians, especially church leaders, seeing in this movement the presence of the Spirit of God.

Culture-Bound Renewal

Culture-bound renewal is in fact a corporate form of fleshly renewal. It occurs whenever charismatics refuse to let the Holy Spirit challenge the prevailing culture, but the new-found power is used instead to reinforce cultural patterns. Instead of the Holy Spirit challenging "the American dream," the Spirit is seen as the most effective way of "making it." Instead of the Holy Spirit convicting people of nationalistic arrogance (whether American, British, French or whatever) and breaking down racial and ethnic barriers, the Holy Spirit is seen as the main architect of national greatness. Instead of the Holy Spirit challenging our inherent greed, our tendency to assess people by their financial value, our insatiable desire for possessions, our desire to impress others, the Spirit is seen as the dispenser of these worldly blessings.

While many people influenced by culture-bound renewal have clearly been touched by God, and many have been brought out of patterns of serious sin and bondage, their failure to see the flesh at work in these cultural attachments seriously limits the renewing work of God. Not only is their ongoing bondage to mammon a counter-witness to Jesus Christ, but it has a distorting effect on the whole Christian message.

Culture-bound renewal is also a major handicap to the international work of the Lord. The Holy Spirit of God brings together into the unity of the body of Christ people of all races, tribes, nations and languages. In the new Jerusalem, we are told, "they shall bring into it the glory and the honor of the nations" (Revelation 21:26). Culture-bound renewal, however, sets nation against nation and culture against culture. Its evangelistic efforts export a particular culture along with its form of the gospel. The unity of the Spirit is then broken down by nation and culture.

Domesticated Renewal

Domesticated renewal is the result of subordinating the grace of the Holy Spirit to existing church structures and policies. It does not allow the Holy Spirit to challenge the central presuppositions of church life. Instead, if the movement is welcomed, it is welcomed as a source of new energy to revitalize the existing system. Like fleshly renewal and culture-bound renewal, domesticated renewal is yet another way that sinful man tries to use the Holy Spirit to realize his own goals, instead of submitting to the Lord to receive the Spirit's conviction and revelation. This time, the goals are the perpetuation and expansion of the denomination or the congregation, without considering how these accord with the Lord's plan and priorities.

Church people can often think that the biggest danger in the charismatic renewal is non-denominationalism, people leaving the historic churches for new independent charismatic assemblies and sects. In fact, domesticated renewal is probably a greater danger.

The greatness of this danger is often not seen because of the extent of our "churchification." Churchification is the process by which church comes to replace Jesus Christ. It happens whenever the interests of the church as institution become paramount, where serving the church replaces discipleship of Jesus, where repetition of formulae replaces knowledge of the Lord and Savior, where letter has taken precedence over spirit. Instead of the church serving and worshiping her Lord and master, manifest as the body of Christ, a churchified church appears as an end in itself and obscures the Lord it professes to serve. In a churchified church, the patterns of fallen humanity, i.e. setting up a world-system without submission to the living God, have invaded the very body professing to witness to our redemption.

Churchification is the mother of division. A worldly church, a church that does not truly reflect the face of Jesus, invites protest and rebellion. The attraction of non-denominationalism is directly related to the unattractiveness of the historic churches. The only solid response to the threat of non-denominationalism is to combat the disease of churchification. Churchification can only be fought and removed by the opening up of all dimensions of church life to the convicting and challenging work of the Holy Spirit.

Domesticated renewal does not see the real state of the churches. It has not woken up to the extent of infidelity and disobedience within the churches. It may think that individuals need the renewal, but the church is basically healthy.

Domesticated renewal is a disaster for the churches and for Christian unity. For as domesticated renewal sees the "baptism" making Anglicans better Anglicans, Catholics better Catholics, Lutherans better Lutherans, Methodists better Methodists, Presbyterians better Presbyterians, etc. it reinforces the historic divisions. Instead of challenging and purifying the elements in our churches that have caused division, and are gravely displeasing to Almighty God, domesticated renewal plays down the ecumenical character of the movement and sees the renewal of one's own church as separable in principle from the renewal of other Christian traditions. Only as the church-centered mentalities of divided churches are challenged and opened up by the Christ-centeredness of the Holy Spirit, can this movement bring its God-appointed harvest.

The Glory of the Cross

Overcoming all these deviations in the renewal is only possible as we understand and appropriate the cross of Jesus. Fleshly renewal, culture-bound renewal and domesticated renewal are all manifestations of flesh (*sarx*), encroachments of the pride and self-glorification of fallen humanity. They are as it were Satan's last foray, attempting to cripple God's own work of renewal with the very disease the Lord has come to heal.

The wonder of Christian faith is that the cross of Jesus has nullified the pride of human flesh, putting to death the roots of sin. "God chose what is low and despised in the world, even things that are not, to bring to nothing things that are, so that no human being might boast in the presence of God" (1 Corinthians 1:28-29). None are exempt from the pull of the flesh. But thanks be to God, we have the victory in Christ. As we are incorporated into his death, our old nature is put to death: "We know that our old self was crucified with him so that the sinful body might be destroyed and we might no longer be enslaved to sin" (Romans 6:6).

As we see in ourselves any manifestation of flesh, any tendency to make God and his gifts serve us, then we have to take it to the cross of Jesus. We have to proclaim, "We have died with Christ," and by the power of the Spirit declare dead every present manifestation of the flesh drive. Then the power of the cross to render null every proud thought will be manifest, and the new creation will be seen in its integrity and purity. "Far be it from me to glory except in the cross of our Lord Jesus Christ, by which the world has been crucified to me, and I to the world. For neither circumcision counts for anything, nor uncircumcision, but a new creation" (Galatians 6:14-15).

CHAPTER THIRTEEN

Relevant Ecumenical Principles

THE SIZE OF THE DANGERS OUTLINED IN THE LAST CHAPTER should not alarm or depress us. They are an inevitable consequence of the fall. While it is essential for us to be aware of the depth of our need for salvation and healing, we also need to know that God's love, mercy and power are infinitely greater than the power of sin and evil. As Paul says, "where sin increased, grace abounded all the more, so that, as sin reigned in death, grace also might reign through righteousness to eternal life through Jesus Christ our Lord" (Romans 5:20-21).

Because the roots and consequences of the fall are so deep in all of us, we all need great humility as we pinpoint the dangers to the Lord's work. In no case are we pointing at sins and weaknesses of other people, of which we ourselves are entirely free. But seeing and recognizing the dangers, and confessing the infinitely greater power of the Lord's cross and resurrection, we can repent of our complicity in trying to harness the Holy Spirit for our own self-centered and church-centered purposes. Then we can all take hold of the grace of the Spirit to glorify Jesus Christ in a Christ-centered church.

New Situation

Before outlining the relevant ecumenical principles that will promote rather than undermine the ecumenical action of God in the renewal, it is worth reminding ourselves that this work of the Lord has created a new ecumenical situation. There has not been in the centuries of Christian division and separation any previous example of one and the same divine grace being poured out on Christians of all traditions across the entire world.

This unprecedented ecumenical grace has brought about a new situation in ecumenical relations. Prior to the charismatic renewal, aside from a small group of ecumenical specialists, relationships between Christians of separate traditions were almost all occasional. People came together in the week of prayer for Christian Unity in January, or to work with one another on some service of charity. Only in a few places had separated Christians committed themselves to regular prayer and fellowship together. When joint prayer was held, the alternatives were either to follow the form of one tradition or to devise a form of service that wasn't anyone's regular pattern. The growing theological dialogue between the churches affirmed that there was a basic bond of unity in common faith in Jesus Christ as Savior and Lord, a bond expressed in baptism, but this unity was not something known from within by ordinary church members. The assumption was that as theologians uncovered common faith ground, so the separated churches would grow in unity. Conscious unity in the Spirit was thus largely a goal for the future.

The contemporary renewal in the Holy Spirit has turned this process upside down! By an intervention of the Lord, those baptized in the Spirit have been brought into a unity in the Spirit. This unity is not complete, for many unreconciled differences remain. But it is a spiritual unity realized at the most basic level of relationships with the Father, the Son and the Holy Spirit. Through this same grace received by Christians of all traditions, they are able to worship God in a new way that none could do before. Their common praise in the Spirit is the deepest expression of this new God-given unity.

The work of scholars and theologians—deeply believing scholars and theologians—is as necessary as before. But it is now to illumine and facilitate the process from this existing unity in the Spirit to full eucharistic communion and unity in the profession of faith.

This new situation of a basic realized unity in the Spirit means that the way ahead cannot be worked out simply by consulting and applying ecumenical regulations drawn up before the appearance of this unexpected grace. The way ahead cannot avoid being a walk in faith. The Catholic bishops at Vatican II must have had some supernatural sense of this truth. They ended the Council's decree on ecumenism by urgently desiring "that the initiatives of the Sons of the Catholic Church, joined with those of the separated brethren, go forward without obstructing the ways of divine Providence and without prejudging the future inspiration of the Holy Spirit" (para 24).

Past ecumenical guidelines do not become totally irrelevant, for there is always a continuity in the Lord's work. But with each new stage of the Lord's call to unity and renewal, the principles to guide the churches will be more and more the principles of basic spiritual discernment by which the promptings of the Holy Spirit are sifted from all other manifestations.

Perhaps the surest guideline would be "Build on what is most certainly of God." God is "the builder of all things" (Hebrews 3:4), the builder of the body of Christ, the builder of the holy temple (Ephesians 2:21), the builder of the new Jerusalem. God's present work builds on his past work. There is no new grace of God without careful divine preparation.

However, this seeking out of what is most certainly of God needs to be a corporate work. It is not me, deciding privately on my own, what is of the Lord, and how certain this is. It is a work Christians are called upon to do together, so that our brothers and sisters in Christ can correct our own subjective biases. However, it is not sufficient that each church tradition separately discuss the work of God in this movement. Being an ecumenical work, it calls for discernment across our church boundaries. One of the sad features of church reaction to the renewal has been the almost total absence of common discernment and response with other churches in testing this work of God.

It is in determining what is most surely of God that we can return to the characteristic works of the Holy Spirit: revelation leading to confirmation of the apostolic faith, and conviction, leading to challenge and repentance.

Revelation Leading to Praise and Thanksgiving

Among elements that are most surely of God are those realities of faith revealed by the Holy Spirit to those touched by this grace. Throughout this world-wide renewal, there are some central realities made clear to virtually all who are hearing the Lord, together with adjunct realities becoming clearer to many. The way to test what these realities are is to work out all for which we can praise and thank God throughout this movement of the Spirit. We should do this, not just to get clarity on the unity given, but also to praise and thank God for this work of his Spirit. For the very act of praising and thanking is the only faith-filled way of appropriating God's grace.

Among the basic realities revealed in the Spirit throughout the renewal are the following:

☐ All people need the saving grace of Jesus Christ
☐ This salvation is only realized through the death and resurrection of Jesus Christ, the one mediator between God and the human race.
☐ This salvation is received through faith in Jesus Christ
☐ Jesus Christ is the eternal Son of God
☐ In his resurrection and ascension, Jesus is Lord of all, having all authority in heaven and on earth
☐ At Pentecost the Holy Spirit of God was poured out on the church
☐ This fulness of the Spirit poured out at Pentecost is available today

- ☐ God still speaks to believers today through his Son
- ☐ The Scriptures are the inspired Word of God
- ☐ Evangelism is a command of the Lord to the church
- ☐ God's purpose is to have a united people who as one body under Christ the head will glorify the Father of all

If these are the realities the Lord has revealed to all truly baptized in the Spirit, then we have an obligation together to praise God for them, to thank him for his revelation, and to make them the basis for our ongoing response.

These truths shared by all across the renewal are more basic and foundational for the Christian life than the things on which we still differ. This is not to say that the differences do not matter. For example, as a Catholic I believe the eucharist to be very important. But I know that who Jesus is and what he came to do are more basic. These most basic realities shared in the Spirit are then the foundations on which we must build. This is not just because I think or others think that these are the most basic truths. It is because the Holy Spirit in his revealing activity has shown this to God's people.

Conviction Leading to Repentance

As the Holy Spirit reveals the Word of God, so the Spirit convicts us of all that is opposed to Jesus and the holiness of God. The Spirit calls us to repent for the ways our churches have not lived by faith, for the ways they have erected other things in practice above the person, the message and the truth of Jesus.

Christians of each tradition need to examine how they have betrayed their call, how they have served "other gods." Catholics, for example, need to repent for neglect of the Scriptures as God's Word, for church-centeredness rather than Christ-centeredness and for proprietary attitudes toward believers and the grace of God that deny the Lordship of Christ. Other Christians may need to repent for other sins, maybe for narrow and restricted use of the Scriptures, maybe for neglect of the eucharist, maybe for individualism. There will be no Christian body unconvicted by the Spirit. All perhaps need to repent for so much talk about renewal and reform without ever getting on our knees to repent!

Though we may need to repent for different things from Christians in other traditions, there need to be occasions when we repent together. This common humbling of ourselves before the all-holy God shows our equality before God as redeemed sinners. We are all unworthy recipients of God's choicest favors. This common repentance will be the surest sign that none are acting as the prodigal son's elder brother, looking down with an attitude of "We were totally right. The others were the ones who really needed to repent."

The next steps have to be based on this repentance. The Lord has brought us together from such different backgrounds. The coming together is his grace. Staying together is only possible through the continuing grace of humble repentance.

Practical Consequences

What are the practical consequences from this shared praise—thanksgiving and shared repentance?

1. *Ecumenical patterns in the renewal clearly begun by God's grace should not be terminated on the basis of a priori denominational principles.* This follows from the points already indicated. It does not mean that ecumenical communities, groups or conferences in the renewal are perfect, and beyond correction and advice. But it does mean that where the initiating work of the Spirit was clearly ecumenical, it is interfering with the work of God to split it up into denominational components on the basis of *a priori* theological theory.

2. *Ongoing theological and doctrinal differences should be dealt with in the context of mutual recognition of unity in basic Christian faith.*

Because this work of the Holy Spirit has brought together Christians from such varied backgrounds, it is not surprising that charismatics often wonder how others baptized in the Spirit can continue to believe what they do. Protestants can be puzzled as to how Catholics can continue to honor Mary as they do, while Catholics can be equally puzzled as to why their Protestant brethren do not believe that the bread and wine in the eucharist is the body and blood of Christ.

Both sides have to be clear about the basic faith in Jesus they share through the Holy Spirit. They have to recognize that this is more important than the differences that remain. However, the points on which other Christians differ should not be hastily dismissed as trivial, nor should they instantly be denounced as false. When brethren in other traditions clearly glorify the Lord Jesus in their lives, the distinctive tenets they cherish should be respected. This is an element in respecting the Lord's work in them. The Lord probably does have more to show them about such convictions, but he is equally likely to have things to show us about the same topic, whether it be the place of Mary, assurance of salvation, the presence of the Lord in the eucharist, predestination, or water-baptism.

When we see authentic spiritual fruit in those baptized in the Spirit in traditions to which we were previously opposed, we must respect and trust the Holy Spirit's work in them. When they praise and love Jesus Christ, repent for sin, cherish the Scriptures, evangelize and love one another, then who are we to condemn them? Maybe they are wrong on some points, but they are not usually wrong in exactly the way we think, for our divisions have increased blindness on all sides. Maybe we should share our concerns with them. But we should expect that the Holy Spirit who clearly dwells within them will continue to lead them into the fulness of truth. To pursue the fulness of truth together is the surest safeguard against inherited blindness prevailing over present enlightenment.

3. *Do not apologize for your own tradition.*

Each tradition that confesses Jesus as Lord and Savior has a marvelous heritage. Each such tradition has its saints and heroes of faith. We should have a proper pride in our tradition, just as we can be proud of our natural families. This proper pride is not based on alleged or asserted superiority over other churches, but is based on gratitude to the Lord for the gifts we know he has given our people. This is true even of those churches that lay claim to uniqueness in being "the true church of Christ" in a way not conceded to other Christian bodies. For that claim is itself based on what people believe the Lord has done; it is not a conclusion based on negative judgments on other churches.

Thus however aware we become in our fellowship with other Christians of the sins of our own church and of our forebears, our dominant attitude should be one of humble gratitude for the work of God in our church, a work that is so much greater than the sin. We should never allow ourselves to feel we have to apologize for our church tradition, nor should we pressure others into feeling they have to apologize for who they are. Humble repentance together will also assure mutual dignity and the knowledge of together being forgiven and reconciled by our common Lord.

4. *Rootedness in our own tradition is more important than detailed instruction.*

There is a tendency for church leaders faced by an ecumenical explosion like the renewal in the Holy Spirit to emphasize the need for their church members to be well-instructed in the doctrines and practices of their own church. The problem with such instruction is that it often presents people with a clarity of doctrines drawn up during the periods of total separation. These formulations were often the most narrow, and the most in need of shaking up by the Holy Spirit through fuller exposure to the Word of God and the most ancient tradition.

What is more important is a rootedness in our own tradition, which comes not so much from a course of instruction as from a deep immersion in the heart of a church's life. This would include immersion in the liturgy for those in liturgical traditions, knowledge of the great Christian heroes and pioneers of faith from our tradition, a sense of the emphases and priorities cherished by our immediate forebears, a sense of how the holiest of our people have fed themselves on the divine Scriptures. This spiritual immersion in the life of a church produces its own grasp of the truths of Christian faith passed on in that tradition.

Part III

CONCLUSION

CHAPTER FOURTEEN

Vision, Hope and Responsibility

GOD IS DOING A WONDERFUL THING IN OUR DAY. ITS GREAT-ness and its magnificence exceed the grasp of our limited minds. Like all great works of God, the renewal in the Holy Spirit is threatened by the self-centeredness and the small-mindedness of human beings. As always, the plan of God is being worked out in and despite our sinfulness. But in his condescension, the Lord entrusts himself to us who are so untrustworthy. In God's providence, so much depends on our response.

This book has sought to describe the greatness of this work of God. It has aimed to bring all the facets of this renewal into focus so that we can see it for the amazing grace it truly is. It has presented the great issues that are at stake as the churches grapple or fail to grapple with this wave of blessing from the throne of God.

The renewal in the Holy Spirit is not equally strong everywhere. In many places it has glaring weaknesses not found in organized renewal movements founded by dedicated and mature Christians. The weaknesses reflect in varying degrees spiritual immaturity, inadequacies in leadership and teaching, lack of understanding of God's work, fearfulness of the divine challenge, attachment to old securities.

But despite all the froth and the dross, the evidence is clear that in this movement the power of the Holy Spirit has unleashed great currents of spiritual life, praise, evangelism and service. The renewal is alive wherever its central grace, the baptism in the Holy Spirit, is cherished and understood. It is alive wherever generous hearts and humble minds place God's gift before personal and institutional interests. It is alive wherever this grace is welcomed as the pearl of great price.

New Hope for the Church

This outpouring of new life through the baptism in the Holy Spirit has created a new vision for a reunited and renewed Christian church. Congresses which gather in the Spirit Christians from every kind of Christian tradition generate a vision and hope for one united church of Christ to manifest the power of the gospel to the world. At Kansas City (1977), Strasbourg, France (1982) and again at New Orleans (1987) the same wonder occurs: people catch a glimpse of the one body of Christ beyond all our inherited divisions.

The new vision and hope do not come simply from the fact of assembling in one place people from a wide range of traditions. The vision and hope come from the new life that these people have all received. They share in the joy of Pentecost. Like the Jews from all parts of the Middle East described in Acts 2, they know they have all been visited by the same grace, the outpouring of new life in the baptism in the Holy Spirit. The vision for the church comes from their corporate experience of worshiping and praising the living God and his Son our Lord Jesus Christ. They know from the Spirit of worship within them that the church of Christ is essentially a communion of those who exalt the Lord. They know their kinship with the twenty-four elders who worship before the throne of God and of the Lamb (Revelation 4 and 5).

This experience of new life is all the more exciting because it is shared with people from other Christian traditions, with those whom we never met nor ever wanted to meet, with those whose name we used to regard as unmentionable. Our new hope is enhanced by this experience of unity in the Spirit. We have been shown by this intervention of God that our divisions are not insuperable, and that the barriers between the major traditions are not irremovable.

This new hope coming with the life of the Spirit is sorely needed by the churches. Who among us is not familiar with the malaise that afflicts the churches—malaise stemming from lack of hope, from cynicism and disillusionment, from a sense of the feebleness of the church against the powers of this world, from a sense of weariness and resignation? The deepest malaise of the church is unbelief. So often we do not believe the message we preach. We are not deeply convinced that the gospel is "the power of God for salvation to everyone who has faith" (Romans 1:16). We say we believe in the resurrection of Jesus, but like the Israelites we often trust more in political power, in ecclesiastical politics, in the power of the dollar. In theory we proclaim that we are saved through faith in Jesus Christ, but in many instances we act as though we are saved by our own ideas, our theological re-thinks and our pastoral projects. How many people go through cycles of enthusiasm and discouragement, enthusiasm for some new idea, discouragement when the excitement has passed, and then enthusiasm for a different idea! In our worship we proclaim that on the cross Jesus obtained redemption from sin and the power of evil; but so often we act as though all the church has to offer is what we can learn from the world, from psychology, from economic theory, from business management. In theory we proclaim the power of the Holy Spirit; in practice, we take for granted the increasing encroachment of the world, the erosion of Christian standards, the decrease in church attendance, a smaller Christian base in each new generation.

It is to this situation of unbelieving churches, of churches trapped in traditional routines of piety and pastoral administration, of churches burdened by obligations they seem powerless to meet, that God has sent this breath of new life. It is significant that in this renewal in the Holy Spirit the vision of Ezekiel constantly recurs. For the prophet saw a valley full of dry bones like the remains in an ancient cemetery. The Lord challenged Ezekiel with the question, "Son of man, can these bones live?" (Ezekiel 37:3). He is told to prophesy to the bones, "Behold, I will cause breath (spirit) to enter you, and you shall live". (Ezekiel

37:5). As the prophet obeyed the Lord, he heard a noise, and the bones came together. As he looked, flesh came upon them. He prophesied again, and the breath came into them and they lived. They were "an exceedingly great host" (Ezekiel 37:10).

Unprecedented Opportunity

Because this wave of the Spirit is an unprecedented grace for our weak and divided churches, it is also an unprecedented opportunity. More is at stake in the churches' response to this charismatic move of the Spirit than with any other divine manifestation that our age has known.

An enormous responsibility rests upon those who have been baptized in the Spirit. The more we understand the special character of this work of God, the greater the responsibility. Where we place the reality and the majesty of Jesus Christ above all other concerns, there the Spirit of God will work in power. When believers get on their knees before the Lord and confess their utter inability on their own to understand and shape this work of God's grace, then the Spirit can teach and lead. When the churches humbly seek out the conviction of the Spirit and repent for their unbelief, their partisanship and their proprietary attitudes toward the gospel, then they will be freed to welcome this ecumenical grace without fear.

To grasp this opportunity of the Spirit, we need to have our eyes opened. We have to see the enemies we face, and we have to know the weapons we possess. We have to recognize the threat of the flesh. It is a real possibility that this work of God can be undermined by the flesh, by the compromises involved in fleshly, culture-bound and domesticated renewal. We have to see our real capacity for infidelity, for dilution of the Lord's work, for human adaptation to make it more palatable. But recognizing all these dangers, we must know that in being brought alive by Christ, we already have the weapons of the Spirit. We have the sword of the Spirit which is the Word of God (Ephesians 6:17).

We have the blood of Christ that cleanses from all sin (1 John 1:7). We have the cross of Christ, by which the power of Satan has been broken (John 12:31; Colossians 2:15). We have the name of Jesus, at which devils flee. Humbly recognizing our capacity to fail, but firmly proclaiming the total victory of Jesus, we can be the instruments of God to bring this marvelous grace of renewal to its full fruition.

This grace is not poured out simply to brighten up dull services, to make us better members of our churches, or to excite people with remarkable signs and wonders. It is poured out to restore God's church to be church after his own mind. It is poured out so that whoever looks upon the church will give praise and glory to the Son of God. It is poured out so that the lives of Christians may declare the truth of the gospel by the way they live as fully reconciled sisters and brothers. It is poured out so that the church can proclaim to a dying world the full richness of the gospel with unmistakable clarity and manifest power. It is poured out so that a believing people may once again cry out with faith, "Come, Lord Jesus" (Revelation 22:20). To him be glory for ever and ever!

ABOUT THE PUBLISHER

THE WORD AMONG US PRESS IS AN ORGANIZATION FORMED to proclaim the gospel message in order to lead people to Christ. Its principal publication is a monthly magazine, *The Word Among Us,* designed to serve as a daily guide to the Christian life, helping individuals and families through daily prayer and Scripture reading.

The Word Among Us is written and published by members of the Mother of God Community, consisting of some 1,200 members located in the United States and Great Britain. The writing is done by a team of theologians, both lay persons and priests. Because *The Word Among Us* is the product of a lived-out Christianity, it is able to deal with the principles of faith in actual practice. By faithfully proclaiming the gospel message, *The Word Among Us* has brought people to a deeper knowledge of Jesus Christ and a more effective response to him.

Subscription rate is $15.00 per year. Write to The Word Among Us, *P.O. Box 2427, Gaithersburg, MD 20879 for details. In Great Britain and Ireland write to Turvey Abbey, Turvey, Bedfordshire, England MK43 8DE.*